THUNDERBUCK

TRANSMISSION TWO

Eye of the Medusa

Flights

XIV	THE 'WHITER SHADE OF PALE'
XV	GARBAGE
XVI	MOTLEY COLOURED CHOCOLATE BROW
XVII	THE 'IMPOSSIBLE DREAM'
XVIII	CHICAGO
XIX	MIGHTY JO YOUNG
XX	FART
XXI	BALD EAGLE
XXII	THE 'CARROT MUNCHERS'
XXIII	FALLEN IDOL
XXIV	FORBIDDEN PLANET
XXV	HEART OF GOLD
XXVI	THUNDERBOLT
XXVII	WICKER MAN

INTRODUCTION

Sequel to the 'Changeling,' this book continues the journey along a path of ever-increasing dark, where the Sun is only ever glimpsed for a fleeting second at daybreak and the Moon extends over all the regions of the Earth. Mathew's quest for truth leads him into a dungeon of despair where the only way is underground. The following pages are all that is left of his work, produced on a defective Amstrad in Grandma's grubby kitchen.

I write these words many years after poor Mathew passed away. His memory will live long in our hearts and his stain on the clothing of all who knew him best.

'By fortune's adverse buffets overborne, To solitude I fled, To wilds forlorn, and not in utter loneliness to live, myself at last did to the horned-one give'

Arian Bumblechook

November 2017

XIV
THE WHITER SHADE OF PALE

A knock at the porch caused the greenhorn to rise impatiently from the wainscot and a break in his solitary star gazing.

He answered the persistent interloper who simply wouldn't see sense and dictated once more to the *cuckoo clock*.

"It's only half past ten," he stated. "That means that you have only been gone for five minutes when I specifically declared the minimum period. I'll play with you later when she has passed water. You can only return when the big hand is at twelve."

Time dangles and the pendulum swings, but still the boy looked puzzled. Why was she always the lucky one?

"Are you blind?" he chided. "Can't you understand a single blinking word?" Stanley had always compelled the little one's attention to detail.

While the three foot tall minikin reclined on the ermine her brother was escorted safely towards the neighbourhood fence.

In the hallway the Joiner's plane and spirit-level angled up the skirting.

Her snow-driven bloomers were hung on a twig of the *vibrant asphidistra* soaring at the weighing scales. Eagerly anticipating the belated guerdon piecemeal the numinous host squirmed and gleamed in thrall-like ways.

He immediately ordered the removal of her dummy. "Good girl Pixie!" he grinned. "Are you going to be well behaved today? What a little treasure you are; Mummy will be proud when she arrives home from the little hours."

"Tail!" she whinged. "Touch him again...will you?" Dash! Dash! He was just about to...

The flat leather football crashed against the garage door and rebounded against the pebbledashing showering its chippings onto the window ledge.

He flogged on the frosted glass.

"Lie across the deck!" he vituperated.

He lewdly lowered his garments once more and resumed the hourly routine in the missionary position.

Her naked matchstick legs opened instinctively as his gorgon penis throbbed excrutiatingly with the iron.

Its bulbous knob jowled assiduously against her scarlet orifice. Never again would his wand of office pulse with such an excess of brazen vigour.

"Nice!" she shivered. "It feels lovely."

She tilted her head from the fundus cloud.

"Put finger in hole?" she asked. His fledgeling twitched.

Pixie twisted the dark strands of cotton elflock between her tiny stubs and removed her other hand from where it had been hugging the greater thickness of his stem.

She placed her loving arm around the teddy bear lying snugly at her side as he paraded full frontal along her length.

"Put it right in there!" she smiled.

Her exiguous nippers raced to fan out her moistened piss-flaps. 'Her clitoris was shining like a runny nose,' he observed. How in damnation at that juncture when she hadn't even started term at the kindergarten.

He glared at her with a shy disapproval.

After only a few seconds he removed the antenna glistening with warm aroma and utilized its properties as a barometer. 'An easterly breeze,' he deemed.

Pixie's bright blue eyes clouded over and twinkled wetly with a grateful resonance. She sucked the bitter pill with avaricious buds.

His bald penis jinked like a marking buoy as she noted the strawberry stain. All good quacks take their temperature?

She toyed sentimentally with the ear of her favourite plaything.

"Rub!" she cadged. "Rub me with your tail until he spits." Where had she got that from?!!!

Pixie was never content to play second fiddle to 'his' sheep's eyes.

Stimulated by her delicateness he leaned forward to
sniff the pungent odour of her puerile
crevice...suddenly the alarm bells rang!

The ridgel hand of Gordon cranked down the tollgate
in their rear.

"Why is she taking so long for a *wee-wee*?" he
barked.

At the same instant his auntie's car skidded to a
halt on the tarmac.

The timekeeper scurried to place their house in
order.

He led Pixie quickly into the playpen wearing only
her shirt top and threatened her with the fires of
Domdaniel.

"No tell-tales!" he sponsored.
She chaffed her eyelid with the back of her paw. With
real tears flooding down her cheeks she swayed and
nearly lost her balance.

Pixie was subpoenaed on the banks of the Lethe that
the *age of innocence* was still on the cards.

The youth bustled her brother out of the room and
ordered him to watch *the deliberations of Dougal*. He
flung on the micro-wave oven.

"No tell Mummy...no tell Mummy lies!" she whimpered.
"Never dare to talk to strangers," he scowled...

Heroin addiction? Temporary abhoration. I can
handle it: identity crisis.

What if she should spill the beans? So many *good
intentions*. Summer holydays. Skeletons in the
cloakroom.

"Have I committed a mortal or a venial sin?" he
wondered. "I'm sorry Jesus...but I hate you God!" he
blanched.

Paroxisms of fear. A vague idea pollinated on the
pangs of boredom...the *lost tribe of Tyre*.

His aunty came giggling into the bungalow while her
toyboy from the playscheme drooped on the passenger
seat. Worn out we should imagine.

"Boys will be boys," she joked.
Esmerelda mark 2 returned with the fried chicken and
her gift of a smutty Aubrey Beardsley.

"Can I get you anything else? There's a kipper in the freezer. You only have to ask."

On the first catch of his maiden voyage he avoided the daemon's rich temptations presented to himself and resigned his lucrative perquisites to old Blinker.

The fun-loving dental nurse fidgeted nervously beside him on the sofa.

Suddenly there was a cry. Mathew heard his auntie call as she fell headlong to the floor clutching the ironing cover.

Lifting her dark head to rest gently in his arms the tentative hero closely scrutinized her baby doll face (like a juvenile lead).

Beads of perspiration formed below her hairline. He noticed almost at once how the top two buttons of his auntie's blouse were undone, revealing the white-plumed cleavage rising and shivering with her breath. They pressed together like a pair of generous twins.

Her buxom load slid unassailably down to the carpet where the plump eisteddfod remained there pretty motionless.

Her red and pouting lips, smothered with a fresh coat of paint, slowly carte-blanched wider, the crust clinging slightly as they parted, and a dessicate dribble of saliva from the corner of her mouth glittered suggestively as he hesitated.

Should he fill it with a bulbous type of wedge? The open hold offered itself seductively to his thoughts as her insensate hand tugged the skirt of his *toga virilis*. He glanced uncertainly over her span where the line of teeth had been ripped asunder. 'That was a fine heap of bullion,' he had to acknowledge.

Still the woman forgot to stir. Mathew fumbled with the rip-cord of her Levi.

Should he just shout for a real life doctor? The wench began to make sounds. Her eyes gazed back into his like a lost echo. She must have been codding all along by the compass of it!

"I've been feeling dizzy all morning but don't let on to Harold," she murmurred.

He woke beside the gas miser with his head buried in the armchair to find the winter gloom had already darkened the living room. Gland fluid had trickled embarrassingly into the crease as Mary and Gretel taciturnly counted the cost. He attempted to disguise the hard-on which always mysteriously erupted, especially on the bus. Squeeze her zits. Chlorinate the looking-glass with scrim.

"Get a move on lazy bones!" she snapped. "My friend is waiting and she's already rung up once."

Dashing for his jacket the "ugly long haired lout" hurried over the threshold. With the 'Best of Cream' tucked underneath his arm he fled from the lair of the pea-worm. He rocked unevenly over the cobbles of the ring towards the large Victorian quintain.

To be honest Mathew had been taken aback by that bizarre story which had reached him on the grape vine.

Apparently she had suddenly decided to scythe her chignon with the dress-making shears.

Pixie had been discovered trying to thumb a lift to town with a trucker. Surely they couldn't connect anything with him? He'd grown shifty-eyed. Perhaps the dye had been cast from the word "Go!"

Wetting the bed, again. Gordon. Mary said.

"Hiya, Archie Passwater..."

"Drugs Overdose!" he stated categorically and rapped on the latch.

The actress of the house offered him a Special Brew from the cabinet in the meantime...

In those days a strange metamorphosis was occurring in the young man. With unwelcome side-effects the youth soldiered on...loitering like a Pigman on the stairs with the lustful water drooling in his funnel and swelling his turgent penis.

By demon theop-neustry he listened fiendishly at the nadir of the shaft to their voices whispering urgently with the pangs of thirst. From down below something rotten gripped the bannister rail with a creak, a cringe and a curl...

"I don't like him do you?" she wailed. "He comes when we're asleep, and stands at the side of our double. Don't go to sleep will you?" she begged him. Her brother assented and agreed with her whole heartedly.

"Put a knot in your pillow and don't forget to look out." Give him a thick ear...

Who was that trembling at obscure heights? Who dared to crouch in the basement prowling deep in the fog? His huge pointed ears flapped like a spanker as he curst for them to slumber and flesh come into season.

With baited breath the white-faced ghoul climbed with extra caution the creaking steps to Eden. His foot hovered above the penultimate obstacle before ploughing over the abyss.

Under the torch in the dark medieval cellar the German shepherd sniffed adroitly at the banana door. She was safely chained below the salon so there would be no 'tender mercies' from her hastate fangs.

Cerberus shook the spectre with a hideous howl. Her groyne was longer than a length of soggy bog paper.

On the level from the fusty pristine hills of perdition the creeping thing scrambled over his mountain pass towards the Green Goddess.

He traversed the Gamehunter's cobwebbed trophies glaring amid the battlements where he was born that chilling night. His eerie shadow humped along the path until he discovered the gem of a second water for which he had been dousing.

Through the eye of a needle Grendel's enormous beak and uncanny grin loomed over the lintel and peered round the cream faced surface of their chamber.

His precedence was followed not long after by his sickly bloodshot eyes and albino palour.

The vile shape-shifter entered beyond the Pale of their portal and floated over their slumbering bodies in the full moonlight to place the powder mirror to her nose. Look behind you!

His silhouette chuckled delightedly on observing the reams of joyous canker (using scotopic vision.)

He turkeyed beside their delicious purring to broach a victorious snigger before mounting the pile of catalogues carefully laid out as part of the course. The familiar perfume which andanted their girdle seemed to torque a flock of seagulls fluttering round his top.

Flinging away the redundant motifs of inhibition he rapidly increased his pace from reef to whirlwind.

Like the shade of a submarine pilot his malicious haunting often lasted for imagined eons.

Grendel 'Noseforartil' breathed a sigh of relief through his quivering nostrils and semaphoring with glee carefully rolled the sheet over Benny's pigment deficiency.

"Come on my beauty," he lewdly whispered and weighed her corpselike limb like a trough.

Foaming at the mouth the lurid Clown with a Talcum mask of white tugged the remainder of the nightdress from inside her anal crevice.

With a faint simper he removed the raven cloak which flowed like a lunar gale around his skrawny frame and danced as if his feet were capped in acid.

Like a 'praying mantis' the midnight necrophiliac leant over the ripe fruit fallen from grace which submissively supined for his obdurate mausoleum.

The sconce of pearl cascading through yonder skylight illuminated his naked body into flakes of rice and flour. White pride, worldwide!

With keen appreciation he discovered Brigitte's genial plasma to be surprisingly warm and accomodating.

Between the gemini knolls of her cushion his cutlass throbbed from the new sensation, clinging to his weapon under the dulcet moon.

It beat seeing her clip-clopping round in high-heels. Any-day.

As his incisors of chalk chattered unstoppably with 'Huntingdon's Chorea' Grendel redirected his glance sharply toward the innocents appealing visage.

He placed his hand over her eyes.

He combed her darling hair with his long goarish fingernails, titillating supererrogatively with the argentine chudder and patting her affectionately on the shoulder with his clammy device, before boring deeper into her behind.

But what was this peculiar tingling sensation germinating near the neap in the pits of his groin? The feeling spread and centred on his glans...as la dolce vita pressed ever more enjoyably into the plump vices of her blistering skin.

His organ peeled back similar to the fleece of ripe fruit. Who in heaven's name ranted in the pulpit and how in Gimle did the Cabalust wamble in the dreamtime.

A teratitical craving deepened into a piston pumping, and before the deviant knew what was transpiring a bounding spurt of jissom exploded from the tip of Gae Bolag.

He leapt in the air like a startled rabbit. The guardian hollered from the nether regions as the planethood moaned southwards.

His skewer showered through all points of the globe. Splattering each article in rapine; the engine running exhaustively until the fuel subsided, the monkey speeding rapturously up the chimney like cork from a gun. "So who's the Governor now!"

Convulsing like pulp in a blast Grendel cautiously returned to scoop up his oil into the rightful capital.

He had a good idea what the emission might be, but by no means was he certain of the connotation.

Scurrying from the limelight the rabid monster discarded his magic talma at the foot of their post where the prints were completely white-washed.

Brigitte stirred and turned over to pull at Benny's share.

She gave a low-key nag and whimpered tiredly until eventually she obtained her desire.

From the corridoor their Dark Angel scouted back and forth on tip-toe. In loco parentis.

Grendel hankered for a chance to rematerialize and sponge away his crime.

Like a sea constantly trying to make its bed he fretted ill at ease in case the couple should examine the snitch baby's under torchlight.

With his garments at half-mast he vowed never to relapse while the house was still blighted and thin at the roots.

The salubrious arrival of their car headlights careering up the drive forestalled the second helpings which this further mumbo jumbo warranted.

Stealing grist from the mill he grubbed the disturbed filaments of the occupation until the inebriate newlyweds entered along the landing.

'Had he been in a hurry from ablutions?' she procrastinated, staring in a downward manner.

The mistress of the establishment relaxed in Fabian conversation while the lambustrious 'Braddock Bull' attempted to stampede her up to slats huffing and puffing in his Boxer shorts.

"Don't get shirty with me!" she railed..."Are you so fucking cocksure?"

Checking that the babes were safe and well he returned with Brigitte who couldn't sleep. She was dressed in her pink-frilled nightdress and her cheeks were glowing with incense. Often had 'bad dreams.'

"Mummy I've just seen a ghost at the bottom of my bed!" she insisted.

Her father assured her that everything was splendid in their turret. The token white gay-guy.

Lifting his daughter for a fond hug from his wife the sleepy-eyed girl was then encouraged to give Mathew a kiss. She thanked him for his fourth dimension until he could come again.

"He's got one just like my dad!" she suddenly blurted with absolute certainty. Oh, crumbs. Husband and wife began flirting. Then the daughter was carried back up the stairs on her father's pigtail.

Mathew reclined beneath her like a scalped royal. "Did we have any unexpected callers?"

"Do you have a girlfriend?" the woman meekly enquired. She seemed amused as Mathew coloured.

"Why ever not?" she asked.

"I can fix you up with my assistant Annabelle." she offered..."Shall I arrange a definite date then?"

"How would you like to begin an apprenticeship in my hairdressing business?"

"She's not pretty enough," he sneered. "I don't fancy her! She's only seventeen and I prefer older women..."

However much he admired the blonde in her short mini-skirt it did not entirely justify the founding of a traditional new sect.

"I'll run you home love," she insisted. "Of course it's no trouble when the Rakehell is over the limit."

They strolled to the white 'Roller' in the silver edged mist, ploughing through the centre of town and into the seedier regions.

"Well, aren't you going to give me a goodnight smooch?" smiled Edwina.

He reached quickly for the handle of the buckboard and slammed down the catch.

Intoxicant! Cyanide of Cythera; corrossive sublimate, tempter God, corrupter of the hundred percent. Why once captured can you never release the milksop?

Even when 'nanna' was called in to replace him many moons later he connived his devious entrance with beansprout. How philanthropic was the magic mushroom!

The 'washer' woman with puckered lips assayed for his erogenous zone as he knelt on the carpet below her thrashing tongue.

She could stroke and fondle his neck while he buffed his gnarled cat's paw over the raised purple ridges of her *varicose veins*.

Alice-Eva pitched like a corsair before accepting the red-hot neve as tolerable. 'Cold hands, warm heart' etc. She whispered like an old tart in a pub doorway...

"You don't look at the mantelpiece while you're poking the fire!" she suddenly counselled. And then..."Many a good tune is played on an old violin..."

What in heaven's name was the fatty suggesting?

Her awry profile just reminded him of *Mother Shipton* as
the bulbous dome shivered over the obtuse trunnion of
the alimentary canal.

"You're exceedingly lucky to have a best friend like
Ryan Starbuck," she enjoined.

The nervous cadet feigned a flimsy palliation to
mount the forbidden string of scales up an extra
storey. Was there no end to this audacity?

"I'm just going to see a man about a dog. I won't
be long!" he promised. His grandmother seemed to sense
a rat was cooking...

The creature sniffed impetuously at their thin red line
as the yellow rectangle below the border revealed they
had not been long hitting the matress.

Alice-Eva hobbled down below as he shuffled urgently
forward with his prayer-mat. The low-flyer pressed his
palm over his mouth to prevent further sibilations.

Under the blistered craters of the argent plane
Grendel 'Brass-hat' executed his meanful trick.

He perused the pillowmorph joined at the hip with
the stealth and hypnotic stance of a bummer from the
black lagoon.

Closing the vault behind him to shove the world of
men beyond he peeled the blanket from his favourite
breeding place. Hard fast asleep again!

Brigitte's cerise and pouting lips offered
themselves to his unbridled lust, but first he gently
removed the restrictive practice of her thumb; there
was no room for foreign objects when Nosferatil's
cartilage ached to stuff itself inside the limited
recess.

With the bluffened pencil-point he drew her breath
while infanta grumbled and protested in her bye-byes.

Hook-nose prematurely celebrated. How peaceful he
would subsequently snooze for once...the rising scent
of their rich bouquet blurred his brain and made his
senses reel.

With an adroit flick of his tool Grendel jammed the
weapon into the beckoning gap.

13

She yawned and gripped his gorgon stem in her mumbling entrance.

She gipped and struggled with his increased tunnage. A line of consternation creased across her brow. Motioning her lips to the rhythm of the wands she tightly squeezed his creaming gondoliers and admitted half his plum by gradual consent.

Throwing caution to the wind Grendel gave a gleeful shriek. He charged once more against her echinate dentures which tickled his oversensitive glans.

While she chomped around his choking trunk he patiently climaxed in a matter of seconds for a full two minutes riot...

The starry eyes of Little Bo-Peep quickly ate their flame as he laid a shilling under her hassock.

His nectar cruised along the crotchet and cascaded over the corner of her mouth before dripping into her ladle.

With obvious disgust she laundered the stub of orts on her sleeve presuming it to be a jam of her own.

Through the candid rails of their cot her large brown eyes rapidly clicked their shutter.

She jumped like a parched pea to discover it resting against the woodwork.

Something in the nature of the beast alarmed her fixed attention. But her eyes could not draw away even slouching on his lap. The family pet laid a lick on his bell-end.

Brigitte grasped her tentacles close against her chin and attempted to break the spell by tapping on his shoulder.

"Go to sleep!" he heckled. "Daddy will be back soon and mummy will be cross to find you still alive and kicking."

He tremoured silently to the bathroom for a cold rush of spring. There was the patter of tiny feet.

Suddenly her micron was standing in the doorway pleading for a drink.

He'd lucre what he could and see if nature careened its seedy course.

There was even an attempt to rebuff his slide between her rug.

Meanwhile an oven fire was creeping up the wallpaper; the supper had caught alight while Grendel enjoyed his spurious banquet in the bowels of the Alpine earth.

He came bolting down the fire escape whipping up his flies. Would he still be committed for arson if he relinquished ownership of their inner sense?

The Iron lady was adamant that if it had not been for his mother she would have called the Flying Squad.

The estranged family had recently retired upstairs when Eileen Fairchild offered to watch the late night serial with him...even though Mary had summoned him early to bed. Riding on the crest of a wave.

'It's far too late in the day for swotting.'
In those Halcyon days she appeared extra grim in the presence of this loving Catholic household although the long separation was still hanging in the balance.
Danny had been moonlighting at wise Arthur Browns.

The four-foot eleven-inch elf curled up happily in the armchair as Carmel proceeded from the lounge to wish them both goodnight. Seventy moons Swalabr.
Never in a million years.

"God bless and give heaven thanks."
She dipped her hand at the door and made a sign of the cross through the back of her bone. Her sister would be returning later from the Ram's head.

Somewhere in time her daughter plunged into the waters of oblivion beside her near relation. Her defunct remains were about to have a close encounter of the Grendel kind it seemed.

Her bell, book, and candle flickered like a sanguine creature as the television screen turned into ether. With a raidate 'ping' the imprint fell dark with his hand on the remote control button. Application tended for growth hormones.

Past like a summer cloud the dermatologically disadvantaged youth had overcome his grit in the ointment.

Uncatchable as the Surrey puma he tamed the hissing babble to focus on the piece of primary lamb...and entered the twilight zone in seven league boots sporting an unfashionable skinhead.

He swiftly assessed the tweed texture of her grey schoolskirt between his fingers before hauling the material slyly upward. Her cover was rucked so far that he could squinny the great beyond. Her pink thighs were riddled with goosepimples.

A slight trace of emotion rippled over her otherwise motionless exterior as he prodded and poked in her levin.

He struck his telegraph pole on the cohering skin of her form and percussioned over the cheesegrating studs.

To reach her mouth drooling toward the flying geese he would have to kneel on the rickety stool. He always rose to the top. The caped-crusader.

Suddenly the back gate slammed and footsteps echoed down the passageway. Fingers tapped on the window where he had forgotten to pull the curtains. Why did he just stand there frozen like a lump of lard? If they caught him he was likely to be struck-off.

He feverishly fished out the keys from the drawer and fiddled with the light-switch.

"I can explain," he coughed. "She is suffering from a clear case of mental amnesia."

Mathew jolted awkwardly to the hatch holding a magazine to furnish his gross embarrass-ment.

The Doctor shook her violently from the deep hypnotic trance and she slowly regained consciousness. But the beast was not to be thwarted...

Hidden deep in the wardrobe Grendel perlustrated the princess as she undressed below the two-tone highlights of the stroboscope lamp.

He peered into the vertical slice of icterus striking down his forehead, and only when her chamber was painted over did he emerge dressed in blue silk gown and turban.

He paused above the pallaver once only for voices
raised in anger to subside once more to calm...

and woke to butter melting on the two tablets of toast.

His eyes skated quickly over her occurance and
casually nodded his absolutions.

Eileen's smooth fingertips had been drenched in the
waters of life.

Not a blotch nor a smear silted her virgin white
epidermis.

She giggled immaculately and trotted gaily from his
room with the tray.

Now a member of the exclusive troupe, the membership
fee of which she was totally unaware...

Lord of the 'flying trip-case'!

£   £   £

'Swallows and Amazons forever'

There was hail shower stunning the opening...it was
four o'clock and the bell had just sounded its spell
down the river. Its ring sent the girls racing over
the slipstream from *Holy-croft*.

She rested her arm on the wire.
"Is it alright if I bring my little sister to play with
you. She's got a new pencil case and wants to see your
puppy so long as we don't miss our bus again."

Mathew smiled. Cross-eyed Mary would be another
twenty minutes arriving home from Temple street. The
sorority dorm had been prepared in ready expectation of
their wager.

From that very first instant he plotted their escape
together and chose rake-boned Stella to do all the
counting.

"Hey, no cheating!" he ordered. "Face to the wall
and do it properly in *elephants*."

With high anxiety he marched the young one up the
winding spiral of the tower. In the *wonderful land* all
dreams could be made possible; that much was certain.
He led the soft and tender thing gently by her hand.

"If a body catch a body coming through the rye," he
chachinated. How did that old song go? "Let's go and
see what Santa Claus has brought you for Christmas," he
jested. Let's play 'Bless your neighbour?'

"Do we have to go all the way up here?" she stilted.
Gerda stood on tip-toe to reach the door knob....the
more distance put between them the better. He could
still hear the whippet methodically verifying her
numbers as he closed the escape hatch securely behind
him. And living right next door to you!

His tongue dragged over the stairs as he followed in
her wake and his breath scorched the roof of his mouth.
The pretty wood nymph hopped those cedar steps to the
top of the world and entered *Hy Brasil* with *stars in
her eyes*. Lord of the 'flying-trap-ease!'

As the twilight played tricks on the wardrobe mirror shadow fell in the early glimmer of the fall. By a slip of fate the *prince of spades* was aided by a fracture of the space-time continuum. The motley youth demonstrated to the miner his *compendium of illicit instructions*.

Garlanded she knelt before the royal personage, the innocent, the sacrificial offering, eager to please and drooping her head as he commanded...ducking down lower towards his lap where the dragon-head rose above the surf like a gorbelly of gnarled oak. The 'Chargeman' tensed as he noted Stella calling distantly below...at the bottom of a well.

"Coming, ready or not...! Are you safely hidden yet?"

Her crackle of musketry plummeted helter-skelter back down the stairs to the sandy embankment leaving them to their communion in peace after admitting defeat with the stiff iron lock.

"That's the last we'll see of the chaser tonight," grinned the overman. He pressed his hands flatly together.

"Shall we say grace?"

A sparse gush of flame groaned from the Gothic window brace nearby as the *Top 'Odd* fizzled squeamishly then gave up the ghost. He positioned her closer to his rule and screwed the words ecstatically from his throat.

"Decant, and slide it through your fingers," he softly stipulated.

Her yellow mop sank deliciously to make contact. She sneezed...

"God bless you!" he hailed. "Remember that your saucer eyes should be shut and your warm hands should be pressed around the hod like so."

She settled for one of her mits, finding it necessary to use the other limb to martial her support.

"Keep your head still," he earnestly directed...he struggled to straighten the deviator whose feather soft cheek rested tentatively against the purple plume of his pimples.

"Now turn your head slightly...no! Back another inch." he remanded. "Put your lips directly over the spot....yes! Just like that!" He brailed his lids and quacked-out gratuitously.

Somewhere in the restaurant 'Freddie' was surveying the menu. "Lower down the drawbridge," he coarsely muttered. "It's open!" she reported.

Should he ask her to perform the ultimate task for her *grandmaster*? Well, he'd journeyed so far, so why not go the whole hog?

"I can feel you now," he felicitated. "Lick the hood and taste the crab-apple." Her sensation rattled the flag. The vertical range of the depth charges were immeasureable.

Her white unblemished cornea loitered over the erection awaiting his categorical imperative.

"Place me in your cavity!" he suggested rather matter of factly.

Gerda swallowed the hulk right up to her hilt and coasted him to the back of her gullet.

But the immediate stampede of horses heralded the emergence of the richly saturated soup alive with cells and vitamins, and that would give the game away.

She suddenly raised her angel head and squeaked. He cursed her frustratingly short attention span.

"I know what this is!" she blurted unequivocably...but it was too late; she'd *swallowed the evidence*! Bad digestion?

"How old are you? What sort of music do you like?" she inquired.

The chinky-eyed manikin with libidinous eyes focused insistently on his hirsute pouch, curiously awakened, and rolled her giant tongue lewdly around the wooden edge of the measuring stick, before penetrating.

Mathew could not help noticing a 'bleg' which had lodged itself in the entrance to her left nostril; although it was not this unsavoury aspect which damned Stella from ever obtaining a visa to his tunnel of love...

He observed with incongruity that the senior citizen
was now wearing a tight fitting pair of blue jeans
inconsistent with her status. He detected a crooked
outline similar to her mother's shabby coathanger of
ribs.

There was a flapping and beating of wings.
Mary arrived carrying her easel with the identical
twins swinging their rackets. One 'has been,' and one
'may-be-was,' it transpired.

"Anyone for tennis?" called Marissa on their way to
the courts. He answered in gibberish.

The manikin was far to plain. Worse than that the
minor girl appeared far too bloody eager...

He listened in the hallway as Mary bellowed down the
phone to her mother.

"Well then, don't send her again," she screamed.
"I'm far too busy and I don't want them here e-v-e-r-y
single night. I've more important concerns to cope
with."

Mathew raised his hands as if he had been held up by
Dick the highwayman.

'I'm sorry but what can I do?' He postured to
communicate in makaton.

Stella pouted sulkily, blushed, and with a wide
friendly grin exposed her finely-chiselled viaducts.

The 'leudes' swooped down from the steppe where they
had gathered round the band-stand like a tribe of
desperate Huns.

Attracted by the distinctive hum of the fan belt,
and the tryst they had agreed the previous evening, a
fresh horde of disciples entered the *Milky Way*.

The *immortals* landed spitting and fighting in the
yard. Who was going to be the first to put their hand
in his pocket this time?

Scouting furtively across the street the *old hands*
gathered randomly in the doorway with the pile of wild-
eyed new initiates who seemed curiously disorientated.

The hazy mob with milkmaid eyes settled like a row
of 'placebo's' for the entertainment to be inaugurated.

Ryan craftily sanctioned the proceedings. It was
agreeable that Mary had been invited to a rally or she
would undoubtedly have been rushing down the stairs for
him to pull up her zipper.

"I've got a monkey tattoed on my chest!" he
chuckled..."If you put your hand in my pocket you can
feel his tail!" he whispered.

Lucinda reached forward to plunge her hand deep into
the cunningly punctured inlet.

"Open your mouth and shut your eyes I'll give you a
big surprise!"

"If you give me a candy you can show me your
'willy'," she said.

The burlesque continued by a process of common
menticulture.

"You've got a bigger dick than him!" ,
The fair young elf blushed at her friends
precociousness and accepted his bribe of the 'Galaxy.'

"Oh, no he hasn't!" protested Mathew: but that had
always been his downfall.

"Do you want to play 'Doctors and Nurses?'"
The scruffy young urchin ran to wave at little Joe the
skipper. Conformed to fact.

"Stop peeping!" he concluded. "Close your eyes
tight shut! Do you want to do the same as Lucinda?"

"Yes, please," she meekly rejoindered. "Exactly the
same."

The passenger instinctively encroached towards his
potion.

"No, not there!" he exclaimed. "Do you want to
cause an explosion? Only further down the stem where
you can sink your teeth into the side."

"She never told me about this part!" Even though
they were from the same regiment?

The Comus grinned. There was no doubting what she
said was down to earth.

His Bobby's helmet met her with a bow.
"Hey! stop peeping again!" he warned her
angrily...well, what the eye didn't see, the mouth
couldn't gab about!

She lolled on him with penis envy flapping her arms defiantly on the up-draft.

Again she rose from the wood. Had she had her fill of board and lodging? Was the acrid odour repugnant to her senses. Don't forget the tickler.

Larissa rubbed the back of her neck and straightened her collar. But life is a roller-coaster ride!

"Can't you do anything to get a bit higher?" she whined. "I like everything else, but all this bending over is giving me a cramp in the neck."

Mathew pretended to strain himself upwards, adjusting his position slightly, and returned to the level he'd already occupied on the toilet stanchion.

"It's the same for me!" he protested, raising his haunches as if he had back-ache. It wasn't anything significant but the effort seemed to satisfy her. She continued to mark the unplumbed depths but he was still much too afraid to extravasatate.

"Could you slurp a bit harder?"
The placebo responded with increased vigour. "I'm doing the best I can," she choked. "I can't take any more of it!" Her eyes sparkled open once more as she did so. As good as his word.

He thought, Oh! damn it! Forget it, just forget it! Then he suddenly spotted her long pointed ears.

The *Comys* was on the edge of a premature ejaculation when he burst into a fit of laughter. For they were brighter than the burnished bulb.

He grabbed the creature roughly by the hair and spurted repeatedly into her *auditory auricle*.

XV
GARBAGE

The school-leaver sauntered to retrieve the mail from dakwallah, and opened the final notice from Alma Mater;

'We wish to remind you that on leaving the sixth form your copy of the Browning version was not returned on clearance day. If this is not forthcoming soon we will have no option but to prosecute. You have been warned!'

Did this mean that a satisfactory reference was in the pipeline?

The Clockwork mouse had accelerated from the catacombed building...feast your eyes on that!

"Don't you think Mathew's rather odd!" a voice was heard to speculate from the staff room orifice.

"His behaviour has been most strange recently." Maurice twisted the finger on his temple and chuckled.

"He's turning into a real Jekyll and Hyde character," he hummed...but one swallow didn't make a summer! "Great job for him," he guffawed. "Down at the poultry farm...taking blind turkeys out for shit!"

One aspect about dustcarts was the bitter taste they drafted in your windpipe. 'Shove that in ya flipping cakehole!' A crunt on the breastplate. Sighed Sid.

Especially on gristswept mornings when the pack of council tubmen ran to starboard as the lead twisted among the cobbled streets ahead. Or hanging on the cuffs like a clutch of bed-rabbits.

Minced with all the foul debris and slurry the *loving spoonful* felt like swallowing a containment of red hot mustard powder.

Every payday when it rained a paste of mud and glue formed upon the face where an impetigo happily festered round the eyes.

A kick from their hob-nailed boots sent rats the size
of cats fleeing from their bread-baskets on the second
layer straight into the iron-mincer's gullet.

With rancorous greed surly General Regan gathered
all the finest mullock; to be weighed in at the end of
the week, and divided among the fortunate few on the
summit of the refuse tip.

"We've 'ad little 'uns before who learnt to pull
their weight. Where there's muck there's brass," he
snarled.

While the crews dashed for last orders the pariah
was still hosing down the yard at half-past three...for
a wage of nineteen pounds.

Up in the messroom they had even thrown him in the
broomcupboard with old Ernie the 'Ratcatcher.'

The heavy breathing faggot had begged to swallow it
in return for a fiver rolled round his...

In a meteor flash the binmen had discovered Mathew
was still a little virgin. Then you could really hear
a pin drop!

"Never been laid?" someone laughed. "Nobody will
ever drop them for old Snozzleconk! Who was it then?"

He turned to ask Mathew if he was settled in his
fond vocation.

"This isn't the job for you lad," he
cajoled..."There's a vacancy at 'Whipsnade Zoo' which
would suit you down to the ground. Why don't you apply
to go training?"

"Wanking Elephants!" screamed the faggot grinning
caustically. "You ought to see the size of their
blooming pricks! Tha'll need a bucket for 'em." But
there were other snags...

"You've been reprieved," snarled the cleansing
department super. "Get ya rubber gloves on!"

Funny. Never had piano lessons like Gretel. Always
poking around in something.

It was usually only drizzling by the time they passed
the affluent 'White horse.'

A terrace of dry stone cottages frowned from the top
of the flagstone causeway.

25

"Come on fucking Mathew!" groaned the old iron driver.
"Don't let Selwyn do all the frigging work again while
I'm mucking-in. You 'aint got time to spend a penny."

From the frosty pleasure garden he carried the leaky
pail tottering over the uneven steps to the *Shitwagon*
grinning on the opposite side of the wall.

The thin steel handle bit into his grip. As he
lifted the pan numerous lakhs of bran began to slide
over his bloodied hand and trickle down his neck...the
whey wheedled through the shaft as the curd churned
with ash and cinders during centrifugal motion.

Mathew covered his mouth and tried not to vomit.
In the doorway the hoary haired spinster smirked adieu
to her stools. Corn on the Cob!

"Nobody likes emptying them there *piss-pots*," he
tiraded; "but someone has to do it."

Climbing in the cabin door of the *Shitwagon* moody
old Selwyn slammed the door purposefully on Mathew's
fingers.

It was a revenge attack for an accident which made
his eyes water.

He returned once more to the primrose path of his
dotage. 'Puts fucking years on you!' he spagged.

Selwyn shook his head regretfully and romanticized
about his youthful conquests when his spike would never
mollify. His spouse had become infarcted with her
second skin. Three score years and ten.

Trundling in through the yard Mary approached along
the street ceiled in her shabby leathers.

"I thought it was a frigging fella when we edged up
really close!" he scowled. Bun-brown wig.

"We'll give you one last chance before you get the
sack. Here's a brush and cart!" said Jack. "Clean
around the marketplace and along the filthy kerbside."

Mathew slowly motored into town trying to appear
incognito...what was he? A Plumber a Painter, a
Candlestick maker? Doing something useful;..thats
fine! Face like the back of a tram smash.

"Have you heard that Moira has gained a place at
Oxford?" she gaily squealed. Cutting up snaps.

But just as he was searching the church green for
public droppings a familiar pair appeared lugging the
shopping.

It beat being loaded in a dustbin and tossed down
the chute by the snoops.

From the direction of the Piece Hall a couple very
similar in age to his mother hitched to converse beside
the lampost.

Mary nattered as if she were stood at her
schooldesk.

He watched in disbelief as the woman suddenly threw
herself into a frenzy.

With hair on end she tore clumps from the wench's
frizzy coiffure, and punched her deep in the mid-drift.

The *human beings* seemed like interlopers as his
estranged sister careered anxiously to the rescue.

Mary's former associate from Bagcraft gleamed like a
Cheshire cat. 'Don't you dare wolf-whistle!'

She continued to lambast her opponent even when the
fight was virtually over.

Mary attempted to straighten up the mistake and
dusted her stumps. She always ordered a pint.

"I can't believe that you're still talking about the
past even today," she flared.

Had she conveniently forgotten leading him on? He
laughed, and *then he called her a 'liar' too!*

"Just look at you!" sneered the barmaid. "You're an
absolute disgrace; whatever did he see in you?" Lost
her hair having a bastard child. She said.

She'd said "Oh! don't be silly! You've had your chance
and ruined it. All you did was sleep all day in bed,
and you'd only do the same thing again. As long as
your housekeeping money is on the table on Friday
that's all I care about. What do you mean you haven't
been out looking for digs?   If my brother Bobby comes
down again to turf you out you know what will happen
next! Why are you always up in your room? Are you
sure that you're not a *Brown and Muff*?"

"Don't make me angry!" chided Mary. "How could you
treat your own mother like this?"

"I've never spoken to my mother like that in all my born days and she's got a damn sight less to be proud of. Don't you dare give your job in without a better one to go to. No son of mine is going to be an idle unemployed layabout! Gretel is sitting *her* retakes."

"At last you've found your true vocation," she sniggered to her accomplice. "I might have known you'd come to no good...he's found his own level." She tossed the poster disdainfully in the container for collection. Another slap on the wrist mi boyyo...

Then Mathew came back to his senses; they were whispering in the front seat. He buckled under the weight. Most definitely into porno.

"We'll drop you just here," he grinned. "Remember, I want all those plastic bags filled to the brim, and no skiving."

They sped unhesitantly down the bank having expelled the oddity in nowhereland.

Dumped on valley road in the middle of a *foreign landscape* Mathew laboured for a while at the edge of the leafs.

He couldn't see why on earth they had tied him to the string of the gridiron waste...it wasn't as if the area needed cleaning very much; all he could find was the *gutter scrofula* which needed scraping-up. Hardly enough for a morning's work, never mind a whole day...bringing into focus. Call him dirty names.

The eight-stone eleven-pound pocket-Hercules scratted through the gum with his prong. Then he sheltered in the shade of the electricity house groove opposite the British Legion homes.

At near on four-o-clock he noticed a young couple moving towards him hand in hand, and recognized them both instantly.

Fatso strutted confidantly linked-up with Genevieve. He showed definite signs of having entered a health farm. Been on holiday.

"*Mooncalf!*" he grumbled. "So this is what you're up to?" He howled at the top of his hooter so that all the neighbourhood could hear.

The cadet was full of sparkle since being accepted by
the Bobbies.

A van pulled up and Cappy drew down the window.
"Come on *Baldy!*" he shouted derisively.

"You've just been reported for *loitering with
intent!*"

When the rank outsider paraded past the archer's board
and into the foyer of the Roxy nightclub that evening
he was feeling crammed with giant optimism; a couple of
tarts pussyfooted at the door to place on their scales
the nuts of each new masculine entrant. A bottle of
fire-water before leaving had nicely done the trick.

As they meandered numbly across the dance-floor Ian
dropped his pin-stripe trousers.

He displayed a naughty 'Mooney' to the grogs in the
upper galleon where they prospered in robes of
sartorial elegance. The third member was reputed to be
as crooked as a ram's horn.

"Don't *you* try pulling a stunt like that or they'll
lock you up in clink," he teased. Ryan had suddenly
spurted like a flagpole. "I could shag the arse off
that!" At first he would appear coy. Then keen.

The cloven hooves of the cattle market herd sounded
heavier than the band as the strutting *'fanfaronnade'*
casanovas ensnared her with a Snowball. She led him on
at first just so she could slap him down.

A conveyor belt of waxwork dummies manoevered before
the mirrors as Ian dribbled slurry down his chin. She
gave him the glad eye. Mathew blundered in his Buzz
Aldrin platform shoes. Shaken not stirred. Three
hours in the offing. Gave her a turn.

"The closer you get the better you look girl..."
blared the speakers. 'Disco Inferno.' Tina Turner.

"Who do you think is the best looking in us four?"
he cracked. "Am I the hound?" sobbed Ryan Starbuck
appearing to rub his eyes in grief. "Why am I always
the ugly one?" he whimpered. He'd never had a spot of
acne in his life. Rutger Hauer lookalike. Distantly
related to Tyrone Power?

'He' looked like 'George.' Who was married to Mildred.

"You aren't!" railed the girls in unison. "In fact you are the handsomest dude in this joint. But we don't like him!" she sneered. "The one with the bent over nose...why do you bother buzzing around with dopey? Little pricks are neither use nor ornament. Alright, keep your 'air on," she assayed.

One and all agreed that Ryan was a very lovely person. Charm oozed from him like syrup down the staircase. He'd charm the birds from the trees. "Never had a wicked thought in his head."

"Have you ever thought of a 'dating-agency?'" asked Ryan resolvedly. "It's the only way you're gonna get a screw if you don't get a move on. I bet you never chat up a bird in here tonight. Never in a blue moon unless I'm very much mistaken. I'll just let them come to me..."

The *odd couple* wedged on the tangent of the palais de danse made long faces...Ryan crooned for the inevitable. It wasn't many minutes until a few approached him giggling from the aisleways. Stuck together like fly-paper. Shite on a shovel.

"You'd be nothing without your big mate!" she scorned.

The girl appulsed who Mathew had been attempting to hypnotise at a distance. Got up in a trendy cheesecloth. Tickle her tummy from the inside. Made her skin crawl though.

"Is that a ladder on your tights, or a stairway to heaven?"

"Excuse me," she scowled. "Do I know you?"..."I don't think so." Accused him of cradle-snatching.

Ryan Starbuck gave his silly friend a bit of practical advice.

"GOOD LOOKS or MONEY are the only things that really count in here!"

"You will never get a second chance to make a first impression. Just go for the one with the biggest tits. It always works!"

"I always let her do all the running. If she takes a fancy to you she'll bend over backwards."

"I don't have much of a personality so I have to rely on my strengths," he insisted. Believed in 'ethical cleansing.'

The body of evidence was based on his own experience...

After her roll in the hay below the walls of Jericho he attempted to palm Julia off on the rebarbative rogue. Ryan had money to burn; he often threw small change from his jacket pocket.

She called Ryan pompous, arrogant and conceited, but that only made his head go through the ceiling. He was an expert in taking the urine out of people.

One endorsement for having bald tyres. Leg in a pot from the smash.

But Mathew had really fallen for her and that simply wasn't cricket. She pleaded with him to put in a good word with no strings attached. Apparently they had the same eyes...

"Whatever you do, don't tell Mathew," she said. The vamp casually emptied the contents of the glass down his shirt and cursed the casualty for when they had been on the Broads robbed of her oats...

Those were the days when Mathew played the field!

Lost in space the time warped youth wandered distraughtly from room to room on the stock exchange...he was turned down more times than a hospital blanket.

"Did you hear about the Irishman who thought Muffin the Mule was a sexual offence?" he joked.

"And what career do you intend to follow?" asked the trenchant secretary.

"He's a 'refuseman,'" jeered Ryan shining a tercid face. "And he hasn't even dipped his wick yet."

She expressed her condolences, even though he *definitely* wasn't her 'type.' At least she would let him down gently.

His deferring movement suggested an untried astronaut walking on the moon. Come on, put him out of his misery someone.

31

"I certainly wouldn't employ that ugly bastard," sniffed the Executive officer. "He's just not that fuckable."

'Now for something completely different,' he thought, as the model shuffled her feet, and hoped it wasn't her he was aiming for. A young man like him ought to freshen himself up.

It was before she was banned for using Monopoly money at the Pile bar. She had even appeared full frontal in the *Levin*.

Candy had never forgotten that dusk in Ryan's beach-buggy. She was horrified to find it was not his little finger she had been holding.

"You remind me of an apple," he gawked.
"What?"...she gasped and pouted like a Barbi-doll.
"*Gold'n delicious!*" he simpered jubilantly. But she still did not give him her full attention.

The wench was reaching for her handbag to disappear to ablutions when he caught her with another original straight from the archives.

"My name's Mathew," he stammered. "I'm supposed to be good at chatting up chicks. How am I doing then... (and, with enunciation) Alright?"

"Do you want to dance?" Her eyes glittered cruelly.
"He's got a nose just like *Concorde*," crabbed her friend disgustedly. "Shut your fucking gob up!"
"Just Piss off!" she hissed almost laughing.
"You're rubbish...stop molesting me."

She pranced forward to report him to the bouncer for bottom pinching.

Why did she always find it necessary to snitch in Ryan's ear lug?

"At least he's got something to be big headed about," she jiggered. Could 'outstare' any silly cunt.

"Take a good look at his face!" she hissed. "My six year old son has a bigger dick than the *Raincoat man*. It's just like polishing the coal scuttle when there's never a fire in the grate."

Fatso had been observing his peerless performance. He arrived on a tidal wave to give the birdbrain his heartfelt goodwishes.

"If it isn't little fucking Moonighan!" he leered. "I
thought they would have had you in the *loonatic asylum*
by now. Glad to see you've still got a spotty clock
though." He feigned to stroke his remaining hair.

And where was the 'Billiard Ball,' jamming cheek to
jowl with the pretty girl in the lebensraum? I bet!
'*Slaphead*' they called him, and '*Slaphead*' it was...

Following a vindaloo at the Taj the lads rovered to the
engagement party at the sergeants. Ryan disappeared to
get his leg over. He'd mowed down a mouser in the
turbulence. She wasn't going to speak to him ever
again...

In a sleek pair of black nylons his wife chatted to
Mathew on the sofa. It looked like a glass of water,
but it was really something much stronger.

He was warily watched by her husband as he sneaked
his hand up her skirt. It was almost broad daylight.
What could he have been thinking of?

"I'm a waste disposal engineer!"
Her husband stared through the crowd but could hardly
lend colour to his prints. Another assault and battery
in the quod seemed imminent. Wait till you get copped.
'You'll cop it!'

Like a raging bull the irate eighteen-stone ex-con
charged across the room to head-but the head-case. His
wife insisted she had not realized where his creeping
hand had been profiting.

"I'd like a word with you mate!" he slavered. He
invited the madman for a showdown in the hallway...but
he was soon a zillion light years away from their
company.

Beaten black and blue Mathew clomped down the stairs
from their bathroom. He hesitated over the final step
and entered the living room with his ears ringing.

"You've been a long time upstairs Sneck," muttered
Tina. "What have you been doing?" In his absence the
boys had ripped-off his dosh and stolen his silver
cigarette-case.

"Nothing!" mumbled the harlequin as he shrunk on the
strand of their rumble scratched by milk teeth.

His buddies kept glancing askance. Ryan gaped towards
his trouser leg. Always said he was a D.I.Y.
enthusiast.

Mathew slowly shifted his gaze...he hoped that he
had remembered to shut his zipper properly. Flying low?

"Thank God for that!" he murmured anxiously. Then
he crossed his legs toward Sally. He flopped lower
than ten ton of whale-shit.

A great glob of semen dripped down his suit flair
after his recent clandestine activity.

A sea of surf was lodged on the outer surface of his
material. Ryan turned a *whiter shade of pale.*

Which auspicious name had been drawn out of the hat
this evening?

Horace from the office?...Gerry the milkman?
That nice man from the Garage who had filled her petrol
tank...or Braddock? His wife was away visiting a sick
relative. Slimey Sid the insurance broker? Ray or
Dick or Colin Creep? Capt. Webb the Scoutmaster? He'd
discovered a way to turn the Sahara over for productive
agriculture. Or Tony Blackhead?

The unmuzzled harlot could amuse the entire squad
now that she had collared a suffrage...all *except the
Pigman.* He definitely wasn't on her menu, and had been
given his marching orders in no uncertain terms before
the fall. 3 chips short of a happy meal.

Shivering with Morton's fork he shinned up the
scupper leaving a trail of keck from the 'parve
componere magnis.'

Even the *Fatgirl* hadn't fancied him.
"Why was your friend blubbering in the back seat of the
car?"

Ryan had other more urgent business to attend to.
"I'm not putting my neck on the line for no cunt," he
expressed.

The 'shiner' crawled his way into the pit. Quiet,
they're coming back; I think you can hear her slinking
over the landing? She entered first to check the coast
was clear, followed not far behind by the Creep still
smoking his cigar.

He'd ditched his ring on the dashboard of the jeep.

"I think he's already asleep...he's always asleep," we're home and dry." You could never really blame a hot-blooded male.

There was no mention of that sordid little scene inside the parish. 'No floor too low to scrub for her.' Slack-Alice.

Aroused by his curiosity the whirr of Mary's sex toy probed through the light tin walls to Mathew's garret.

He closed his proser studs and prepared for the crescendo with hands pressed tightly round his lobes.

Orgasm after glorious orgasm rocked the rejuvinated woman. She climaxed repeatedly and gripped the wooden headboard.

Her bed rattled noisily across the numdah like the skull of a pneumatic drill. A family heirloom regularly employed.

Sighing grandly she begged him to stay the night even though half the neighbourhood had already been woken.

Hidden in the props his garlic smell of 'Brut' grafted the tormentor to her ageing feminity.

Beneath his sheets the *Clypeus* twitched like nobody's darling...never even thought of turning himself in!

XVI
MOTLEY COLOURED CHOCOLATE BROW

In their tiny tenement below the summit of the town's new tax centre the gang of hungry workmen slammed their fists down on the slab.

"Hey there, Smelly!...you're slipping away earlier every day...so why aren't all our mugs rinsed out and the tuck on the table? Joe wants to know how many years it is until you retire. How old are you anyway, sixety-four? You'll still be in this job when you reach the bitter end," he conjectured. "Hurry up you dozey twat-head bastard!"

Their 'mate' in the piping-shed recited an incantation...He emptied the slops over the rigid organic remains in the kettle and said nothing. Having already brewed his own char he gave it a little stir, and rushed along the planks with his widow's mite at arms length.

As he entered the dusty old cabin the packed crowd were already starting to riot.

Had he "been for a crafty wank in the basement?" Drinks were served luke-warm from a lingering spout of smog. 'Didn't think his balls had dropped.'

"What do you call a coon wearing a balaclava?" asked Tim. "Anything you like, cos the cunt can't hear you...and what do you call a coon with a machine gun in his hand?...Nasser!"...even the gaffer chortled at that one. Completing the crossword...to egg-on - toast!

"Hey, Joe, look whose here with the grub!" sniffed Tim. "Nice body, shame about the boat race...where did you, where did you," he sang, "Oh! where did you get those spots, Muldoon. Well?" he grinned in anticipation. "Well, did you find it?"

The shifty-eyed stooge managed to remain silent between the carking lot of them.

"Aaaagh!" sighed Joe rubbing his chops in a satisfied manner. "I had a really good jump last night...how about you Mathew?" All the workmen nudged each other and winked; this was the prime time for the hammerheads lampooning to begin and trigger his blistering prickly heat. Joe lovingly stroked his multi-coloured moustache with fake affection.

"You know how it got like this don't you?" he gleamed..."Muff-diving with the wife on a Saturday night. She's got a clit like a red hot poker!" He bellowed furiously and smatched the air with relish.

The workmen carefully watched to see if their sport would start to blub today. "Look!" someone cracked, pointing rudely at his humbling. "You are blushing! Why are you blushing?" he demurred. "You are!" he exulted. Red-hot-twopence.

"What on earth's the matter with you...is it your heart? Have you got *high blood pressure?*"

As Mathew began to lift the sardine sandwich tentatively to his gob Tiny Tim stood beside him with the builder's tape measure. There were scratch marks on the back of his hand as if a squirrel had been clawing. Another searched his spine for insertion of the clockwork key.

"You could make five of ours from the stuff that's in yours!" he whooped. "Have you ever thought of using a demolition team to blow your snout to pieces...Ha! ha! Did you not realize that you're right shoulder blade is higher than your left?" he junctured.

"I know who he looks like!" snapped one of the backstabbers, holding aloft a copy of the *Levin*.

"Cardinal Basil Hume!" That sent them rolling over the shed. The gobby bastard!

"Go on, tell us the truth then shorty," jabbered the Gaffer. "What do you think about all day if it isn't screwing, or do you play with your nuts when you get home and are lying down in bed? Er, how big is your dick really, just as a matter of interest? We've seen how easy you press the potato weights overhead, so why don't you have a regular *piece of cunt* to shag?"

Tiny Tim jumped from his seat to mimic the Swapper's self-conscious gait as he negotiated the building site rubble. He reckoned to trip over a scaffold pole he hadn't seen in his path. Barney Rubble!

"You know. I'd love to see him on the job. I just would....if he ever gets a solid stalk-on that is!" He burst into a loud and obscene guffaw. "She'd suck 'im in and spit 'im out," he declared. Whatever turns you on. If you've got it flaunt it.

"Boy, but I can't wait until I get home tonight!" he revelled. "I'm going to shove it up her arse just so she can't sit down for a week! It's not how big it is, it's how you use it!"

"Stand up while we measure how tall you are," demanded Tim. "Precious McKenzie was little too, and he was powerful with it."

He pretended to scrutinize his head. "Hmmm! lost a bit more since yesterday. Why don't you wear a wig if it worries you so much?" he asked. Joe cunningly disturbed his dome with a dexterous sweep of his arm. Grab him by the short and curlies.

"I bet his sink is full of molting hair," jibed the older cognate. "Can't you take a joke? We're only knobbling, god does he bite easily. His tash'll never grow in the shade."

The stiff wooden puppet retreated into his familiar carriage...then they uncovered the pad in his boot.

"Look at you, the way you are...are you 'simple' you ugly cretinous dork?" he bawled. "If you fancy a pop you better make your first punch count."

"Grass doesn't grow on a busy street!" he mumbled half-heartedly. Get a rise out of him. Get a pair. Play on a flush. Skin cream like *Diarrhoea Spivak*.

It was Joe who first noticed the tide mark round his cup. "What did you make this from, dishwater?" he hissed. Kick him in a place the sun don't shine!

"Witch's piss!" screamed the Pumpkin eater, as one by one the workmen slung their pots through the open door and into the sun drenched savanna. Flash the ash. Flick it in his bristles. It's how you use it!

"Pooh! You don't half stink muscles. Don't you ever change your socks?" he gasped. Suddenly they tumbled out of the portacabin.

A greasy brown carton was tossed under the table and the door was slammed shut as the beetle-brain sat locked in the dark. He listened to their yells outside the hut from where the *smoke bomb* had been propelled. A cunt had some uses afterall.

The bank of thick yellow fog wound around his ankles as he anticipated his indecent antics before the riverbank...

When the kink returned to the house Mugabe had already finishing flailing his tooth-pick, and was preparing to put his feet up. That cold stare was a warning sign, and Gretel had a complacent turn to her cheek. He'll take you to the cleaners. Married women were always fair game. Five year olds' already in films.

While Mathew hovered over his dried bread and dripping the dry-eyed medicine man scowled with derision, twisting his *swaggering* dreadlocks reflectively in the maw, and bugging the square-shooter for signs of brinkmanship.

"So you say you saw Steve with another woman on his arm in the nightclub?" she nattered...Mugabe concentrated intensely on his lame dog with looks to kill a convict.

"You liar!" she spat. "Steven would never be unfaithful. You're fucking history."

"Well, actually, there were two of 'em," he grinned. A sterner expression than before crowded the chocolate metoposcopy. The head perched like a rotten coconut began to steam from its ears. His eyes began to pop. Look out son! Here's Johnny...

"Hey! That's my boyfriend you're talking about!" she hooted. You know how she worships the ground he treads on. "Admit it! You were wrong!" she said. "Shit stirrer. I hope you get your come-upance. I'm beginning to think the old cow was right about you."

"What i-s he on?"

The woman suddenly burst into hysterics, and her boyfriend had to hold her back in case she spoiled him.

"It's not a question of kinship," she fumed. "Blood loyalties mean nothing to me! You should judge a person on the sort of character they are, not the colour of their skin." She squeezed his padded thigh. "He's just a warped little sadist," she grinned. "And a filthy sex pervert!"

Mathew was just going to say something different when his sister cut him short.

"You wimp!" she pilloried. "We know that you're just no good with women."

He was going to say 'but don't you think that all men have the capacity to behave upright.'

"What about *black rights*!" she clamoured. "Society has failed the oppressed minorities in the matter of life and death. Look at the situation overseas. There are our obligations. Well, at least he isn't going thin on top," she sniggered. "It's highly immoral to discriminate(etc)."

"Such a nice young man!" Mary concluded. "Mathew leave this room at once!" she ordered. "You've caused enough trouble here for one night!" Admiring her sculpture of the bushman...

As the delinquent crept by Second Avenue he saw a walker from the dim and distant past edging down the road towards him. Perhaps help was on the way then?

She stopped and paused for breath resting on her cane before muttering vague reproaches to the wind.

So frail, so frugal, yet so enduring, the sprightly griddle had confounded expectations to receive a telegram from the Sovereign.

In her succinct and sugar sweet utterance the *woman-child* spoke to him as if the intervening years had brought but little change.

"Hello, Mathew love," she euphonied. "It's been a long time since you came to see me. Why don't you pop round one day with Gretel?"

"Do you ever see your dad these days? Eeee...he was such a handsome lad. We felt so proud. I remember when he first came to lodge with us before he got hitched."

"Have you seen him recently?" she asked.

"You were such a sweet little boy," smiled the trow-woman. "I've still kept the first poem you wrote at Saint Sebastians; 'Fairies on the surf' You won't remember my husband Jack...are you doing a bit of courting yet?"

As he traipsed by Oxford fisheries the fully grown hoodlum approached him from between two parked cars.

The head-hunter curled his lips and flashed his teeth as he offered Mathew his clasp.

A queue of onlookers outside the Bingo Hall had ringside seats as Steve Mugabe let fly.

His first blow knocked Mathew clean off balance. Then the martial arts expert set on him with a further flurry of shots which sent him crashing against the cordon.

"*White Trash!*" he shouted. "You're a fucking freak! I'm going to turn you into gingerbread." He clocked him on the snout with the ridge of his knuckles.

The *aspiring pimp-and-lawman* continued to supply Mathew with the thrashing of his life until he had him laid out on the ground for a further sting of his brogue.

Knocked the wind right out of his sails...Said he would. Said he could.

During a lull he managed to scramble to his feet and take it on the chin.

Hobbling down Victoria road with his mutilated platform heel he begged for mercy from his pursuer. A spirited fightback gave the pusher an added bonus.

Running like the clappers and shaking like a leaf Mathew flew in their front door and quickly bolted it behind him.

He pounded up to his room where he fretted in the tar-barrel with a stink plugging his nostrils.

"How dare 'you' lock my door!" she screamed. "Who do you think you bloody well are?"

They invited the *good example* into the honeymoon suite. He was gleaming victoriously, almost mocking, and bragging it had been money for old rope. Bees round a honey-pot.

With true love, patience, and understanding Mary ran
to..Steve Mugabe, and flung her arms around his neck to
ask if he was out of breath. Gretel hugged his other
shoulder and had a crafty feel of his weapon. In her
new black-and-white frock.

"Well done!" grinned Mary. "He's had a good hiding
coming to him for a long time! Let that be a lesson.
How could he expect otherwise...and there's another one
coming in his direction. He's just a bloody racist!"

The maggot's heartbeat had frittered considerably as
he cottoned-on to their footsteps, stomping noisily up
to the place. The ultracrepidarian intercepted his
brutal foreplay...surely their heads could nearly be
squashed by an elephant's paw.

Then the telephone rang just as Lora-Lee was
standing against the wall. "Close your eyes and take
deep breaths." She was firm for her brood, but not
particularily for a daughter of Adam.

"All alone?" giggled the Fatwoman. "We'll have to
meet up one full moon." Wouldn't touch her with his.

"You can't make a silk purse out a sow's ear," she
pandered. "But I have one or two things you might find
interesting."

For hours the primary school teacher chattered and
grunted. The claver of lips shrivelled his scheming
proboscis.

After finally giving her the elbow he cut the wire.

'She' was crying when Mary answered the late night call
from her flat. He'd never heard her sob before and it
sounded quite pitiful on the extension.

When she mentioned the word *dentist* his heart
skipped a beat. Mathew realized the pretty elf must
have told her everything about the knitting bee.

"I've never seen her in this state before. You're
son must have put the fear of god in her," she said.
"Should I call the station? She's bawling the whole
house down." Jody, head-in-the-air!

"Stay right there!" loured bloody Mary. "Don't do a
thing until we get to the bottom of this."

Trust his luck to be nabbed on a perfidious line of questioning.

Then he distinctly caught the *renegade* attempt to describe his organ-loft.

Fortunately she recanted and burst into tears again. "No case history!" Close escape? Phew! But don't count your chickens just yet..."I'd only taken her temperature."

There was a hard thud on the wood and the dark foreboding presence of the *Marshal* passed over the threshold with his greeting card.

Though he was not dressed in black a fowl of mourning disfigured his Judas kiss.

He was offered a seat in the living room so he could go into details. Bit of a bright spark.

"We have received an urgent message on the transmitter," he issued glumly.

"A local Catholic priest recognized your son being involved in a very serious incident. Apparently there was a fracar outside the bingo hall."

"I've checked with his former Grammar school," he flushed.

"They say that Mathew was not just bright, but very bright," he gaped. "We take a very dim view of brawling in the street and Mathew is lucky he is not up for *disturbing the peace.*"

"I'm sure they must have switched cots at the hospital...you do bring shame on me." She gave him her blackest look.

Then she whispered in the *Marshall's ear...*"If I have any more trouble can I count on your assistance to evict him?" She pleaded helplessly. "I'm sure he is heading out of control."

"I suppose I will have to do the best I can with him." She bowed and shook her head regretfully.

"At least he's found a steady job to aid clearing his name! There's never been any sign of it in 'our' family," she fumed.

Tall and thin rose to vacate the establishment and was gratefully passed his hat and coat.

He said 'pull yourself together,' she said 'tighten up your clockwork.' His powers of deduction were out of this world.

"I've had a word with my super. We have decided *not* to press charges - on this occasion..."

Sometimes when she weeps, she thinks the worlds not fair...and sometimes when she cries, she thinks that no-one cares.

He'd wanted to be free; to sow a few more 'wild oats!' "There's plenty more like you," he'd scorned, "who want to go the distance." But there'd soon be another following close behind...

Since the embryo had been annihilated her lover had departed...deserted, the plucked pidgeon lies with an empty vase by her bedside...and stabbing pains in her abdomen.

A stretcher-bearer holds her fevered hand to the watch.

The woman arrives to play at loving mums and daughters.

But it's all a farce! A dirty rotten sham. There's soughing in the cough hall...'Would she be spared?' she asked.

The after-effects of *Paracetomol* can be quite grim even in the prime of her life.

The colour of death she dappled the softness of light.

Her taciturn visitor impersonated the correct bedside manner on such an eleventh hour.

She decided to give him the mushroom treatment; keep him in the dark and feed him on fertilizer.

"Should I tell buggerlugs?" she torpidly mused. "So far he's totally ignorant about absolutely everything."

"Don't tell him anything at all!" she spluttered. "Mathew's not my brother. He's nothing to do with me!"

XV11
THE IMPOSSIBLE DREAM

Ever since that vacation visiting the naturist colony at Torcross, Julian Biggs had been prone to expose his 'Baby's arm' when 'over the limit.'

The blotchy beanpole with a wiry-thin physique, and pig-like snout, crowed over the increased status which this new notoriety brought him, though he never forgave his two persecutors for feeding him *dog meat* from the unmarked can at the camping stove that long hot summer.

His prolific stock and trade, apparently a family trait, began to alter the quality of his entire co-existence.

His irascible integument angrily reddened in the stream of light, to bake still further in the blistering and damaging rays, until three hours later they roused him to take a gander at the enormous *emerald* freckles smeared across his skrawny shoulders.

With his discarded wench sunbathing on the rocks Ryan Starbuck contemptuously threw pebbles on her midrift...standing alongside Julian flexing his muscles like the before, and *after-math*...he had decided not to remove his trunks. She eventually took the hint, burst into tears, and roared off in her Triumph *Stag*. When *Sarah* was gone they focused on the exception, and mocked poor Julian's big toe which Ryan said he would have been proud to deploy during *sexual intercourse*.

Julian's mother, a local Yoga teacher, had confided in the bleached blonde Adonis...

She begged Ryan not to tease her teenage son about his appearance any longer if he valued his friendship. Apparently he had been having nightmares about Ryan stealing his girlfriend. When he had one.

On his first day at work, as a Park keeper mowing the *Sanitarium* lawns, the tall gangly *Biggs had* managed to chop his big toe clean off.

He was rushed straight into *Outpatients* with the bleb
wrapped in a bloodied handkerchief.

The novice began to take lessons from his idol in
the art of 'taking the urine...'

Ryan could mount two in quick succession. He said he
would probably never 'tie-the-knot' though.

He pretended to preen his hair in a fictitious
looking-glass held in his hand.

No woman had ever failed to achieve orgasm when he
was planting the crop.

His prick had always done its duty even when he was
the prime candidate in a rough and tumble gang bang.
His mother never failed to sing his praises. He had
recently proved his claim that such a handsome rogue as
he could use *bestial force* with impunity.

"By laughing at someone else's misfortunes, we can
best learn to laugh at our own," Ryan remarked.

"If you were ever inferior in something you will
always have a complex no matter how much you break with
the past," he admitted.

"Anyone who doesn't take someone on *face* value must
be extremely shallow...Bobby Charlton would never get
selected these days. Even if he played like a dream he
could never be the subject of schoolgirl's fantasy."

The great Ryan himself had once been called a
shrimp. His T-shirts were always allowed to shrink.
His mother refused to let him go and travel down-under.

"You'll be lucky if you manage to make one or two
genuine friendships in a lifetime. Don't even trust
your own brother. One man's tragedy is another man's
gain. It's not the taking part it's wearing the crown,
and romping home." Nights were spent locked in arm-
wrestling at the bar. 'Would pumping iron work for
him?' he asked. "Will I be able to knock-off Miss
World one day?" But the penny hadn't dropped...

"Just imagine if you didn't even know how to toss
yourself off," winked Ryan. "It would be impossible to
know how to use it properly before the dinkum oil came.
Get out in the fresh air and sunshine. That'll leave
not a rack behind of your ugly zits Popeye."

Bunny had already offered them the barn for a kip as they fagged around the drinking table after rambling to *Buckden Pike*...

The deep sea diver besieged Ryan to '*Sham the Ram*' again since it always had the band in stitches.

But Ryan could not perform when anyone was watching him. He waited until the packed audience were turning a blind eye before attempting his ace in the hole.

A child's baseball cap which the gifted mimic insisted wearing was pulled down tight over his head. He continued grinning as if he'd just been taken out on a joyride.

The assistant herdsman mulled silent as a lamb with his wild infectious smile growing slowly more animated. His huge pectorals braced and tensed... then, just when they weren't expecting any such drum his lungs discharged a bass vibration which shook the glass from their tables.

Rising on the surf the tide of laughter spread infectiously round the *midnight congregation*.

"Baaaaa!...baaa!" churred the rippling chords once more.

Then with a brainwave of improvisation Ryan duplicated the echoing bleat of a Ewe, wandering lost in the fog across the fenny; the fiery audience erupted into another spirited cachinnation which vibrated beyond the burning stove.

"Cut it out!" entreated Froggy, whose face was turning mulberry. "You're making my sides ache! I can't breath anymore!"

The deep booming fathom emanating from somewhere near his tonsils was so realistic that you could have sworn there was a real *Ram* hidden somewhere below the tap room.

A student of dernier cri rubbed her nose against his as she asked him to pass on his digits.

He placed his hand over hers and then apologized. Never-never-land. Crossed purposes. Trick of the sight. They say.

"Oh, I don't think he's so out of the ordinary," she mused.

"You hardly ever see him with anyone respectable. He's nothing but a self-opinionated bucko!"

"Has anyone ever told you that you have the bonniest blue eyes?" smiled pendulous melons.

"But I intend to be *absolutely perfect*," insisted Mathew. "I've always wanted to be the cock of the walk."

Then Bigsy went and spoiled it all by drawing attention to the size of her *Ibis* beak...

Lumbering up the galley past the old cafe the mixed party paraded back to the Youth Hostel at after one in the morning.

Margot alighted at the brow but he wouldn't go inside for coffee mate. Ryan was disgusted. Apparently 'his' father had been something of a 'Ladykiller...'

He dead-lifted the side of his jeep with everyone crammed in the snood...those rude words drawn by the *imps* on the rigging had become practically invisible.

He'd even been prone to shouting 'Cripple' through the window. A coat-hanger served as the ariel.

"I'll rip his flipping coconut head off if I catch him!" he promised. "Why don't you get out and push!"

The pock-marked trull from the annex suggested climbing in through the lady's lavatory.

To hoots of *Sherwood* laughter they all followed in a chain in case the weather took a turn for the worse.

As the *motley crew* filed cautiously into their dormitories the 'bit-of-a-charmer' pushed her up against the cubicle wall.

He'd sworn never to wear a 'French letter' and certainly kept to his word. Soon it was Mathew's turn to 'dip his wick' in the dark. Down to her whalebone. Beast of 'Old MacDonald.'

"It's now or never, or you'll always be a bilker, Pops..."

"Are you sure you haven't done this before?" he asked repeatedly.

Her pointed teeth drilled into his flesh like an extinct *Bird of the Plains* while Ryan coolly drew on his Dunhill...

- - -

Pleas to mash more gently were contemptuously denied, until someone turned a light on and huzza pelted down the passageway.

"Who's that? Is anyone there?" called the bronco-buster...

"I wish you'd hurry up!" she screeched. "I'm sick of trying to screw this useless oik."

As the ball-breaker rose from the gutter she vowed to inform them of his *virgin incompetence*.

"What an Achilles heel!" And they said the devil never changed his melodic lines.

He struggled for the latch with the monarch bleeding profusely. What a place to give a lucky 'hickey' the refugee conceded. Bit of a dark horse wasn't he?

Racing rapidly to his bunkbed Mathew threw himself in without bothering to get undressed, throwing the sleeping bag over him and pretending to be deep in slumber.

"Let's just try it once and then forget it!" suggested Ryan...

The warden marched out of the porch and snatched the brush and shovel roughly from the Fools.

"Don't bother coming here again," he vituperated. "I do not think that you are Youth Hostel material. You are banned!"

As they walked down the lane Ryan Starbuck stripped to his waist.

Dazzled by day. Could swim like a fish. Had an iron clamp grip over his state of affairs...

Could roll his eyes like a Catherine Wheel. Composed of the particles of stars. Loved by the optical lens.

Crossing the river-bridge a group of cyclists spurted past like a flock of *wild geese*.

As they rose in their saddles *yellow-back* motioned towards the bronzed hulk peeling away his final inhibition.

"Good God! It's Garth!" he jeered, which only made Ryan's head swell even larger...

Bigsy said the *Fonz* could get *any* bird he wanted, but Ryan disagreed...

"If I do get reborn," he joked, "I'd like to come back short and fat; at least if they didn't agree with my opinion they would tell me straight."

"Do you remember the day at Buckrigg Brow?" asked the late-developer. "How long ago is it now, six months?"...had it really been the birthplace of such a bell-ringing?

They speculated about that moment when the reigning Mr. Universe was placated in the ordinary wooden chairs below the ring of coloured lights. Jealous as hell.

The rival American gave his four hour lecture on the *new philosophy* while his attractive young wife waited coyly in the wings. Never had a single grain of sand kicked in his face.

Sitting relaxed and confident before his audience the articulate and intelligent suzerain was not so massive as the other, but had finished third that year due to his poise and natural posing skills.

Steve Adonis declared that there was no real substitutefor *Pumping Iron*.

"The *more wood you put on the fire the greater the flame*," commented the pedagogue. "The higher the load the greater the temple of fame. Healthy body, healthy psychic organism."

He went on to discuss the importance of Amino Acids, and bulking-up on protein. Supersetting and burn-outs, strict regimes. The danger of overtraining; split routines; getting ripped. Reaching for the elusiveness of *perfection*.

The unnecessary use of *anabolic steroids* which he had managed to repudiate; a credit to his methods. Their introduction ended with a brief penultimate question and answer session which was well balanced and informative.

"Have you ever taken drugs?" asked a rough diamond. "How many times a week do you masturbate?" replied the host...

"Now I'm going to pose for you!"
His fans warmly cheered as the muscleman disappeared backstage to transfuse wild-fire in his veins.

After about twenty minutes the well-known signature tune began, and the tardy curtains were pushed aside for a strapping *young God* to take centre stage. The world came tumbling down...

Amid a burgeoning sense of awe the supremely sculptured body mounted the platform of a plain wooden boom as an astonished gasp sounded from the gob-smacked multitude, cursed by mediocrity.

Transformed in his nakedness the *physical culturist* displayed his versatile wares before the spellbound converts: contrasting sharply with the dilapidated interior building of the *old cabinet*. Nature had certainly smiled on him. *Pops* stood about as much chance as a snowball in Hell. Ryan went berserk if you so much as mentioned his calves!

The bunching tissue of his thighs and calves threaded like a sack of freshly strung grapes; the whippet which struggled to be free from his chest; the magnificent striations when he tensed his squamous triceps behind the V-shaped retinue of steel...every aspect of his Everest was demonstrated from each angle, as the grateful complementary clapped and applauded each new variation of a chiselled burin.

Dazed and confused they acclaimed him in long eulogy until all their fevered hands were numb and cramp convulsed their arms.

That climacteric afternoon both Mathew and his friend were captured and enslaved forever by the *Impossible dream*. A chance to kick the ball himself.

Three times the triumphant *magician* returned for a glowing encore summoned by their pious chant...and thrice the tearful audience nearly brought the house down with their ecstatic drumbeat of plumage.

A flood of warm emotion filled the town hall as emphatic new disciples struggled at the rear for a glimpse of the classical Athenian.

"What do you make of that?" he asked, in a hypnotic trance-like state, munching his dessicated liver.

"Well, it's certainly something to be proud of," said Ryan Starbuck. "In any case complete perfection is a very rare commodity."

XVIII
CHICAGO

When Jennie retired to ablutions the guy in the
pinstripe pulled up a chair. 'Typical of the clientele
who frequented the *Muff-diver!*' he thought.

"That your bird mate?" he whistled. "She's a bit of
alright then." Was she a supermarket commodity?
Perhaps her packaging had been brighter than he first
realized; in retrospect it may have been wiser to
introduce her to a wider circulation.

He noticed Jennie returning through the smoke-cloud
of Yobs in a slough of despondency...

"What's wrong with you Mrs. Glum?" he asked. "Has
your cat just died? Is everything okay, twinkletoes?"

"Of course," she insisted, "but could you stop
burning me with your cigarette everytime you move. Do
you have to have a fag? I would have thought it could
interfere with your training."

He smiled and attempted to inject a spark of
nostalgia into those dour proceedings...

"Do you remember that night at the *Ram's head* when
the landlord emerged round the corner only to see your
hand in my belt? He dropped the wine glass he was
carrying. And that afternoon in the development area
when we were petting against the desk....after twenty
minutes we looked up to see X-Ray Buck's study group
with their heads pressed against the window on the
third floor. Didn't we split our sides. Like two
tomatoes! Did you hear about his American campaign by
the way? I felt very close to you in those days..."

She looked kind of sad. "You asked me not to get
too keen, that other girl, you liked her too?"

"Do you remember the sweet little charmer...Kath,
Kathy...yes I did rather like her, but she wasn't like
you..."

"Are you sure that you like me? I know that we've
travelled this route?" On the eve of St. Agnes.

52

But I simply have to ask for the last time. Did you do it before with your other girlfriends? How many times?...Are you sure? Absolutely certain...

"Don't keep on!" he clammed. "It will be alright on the night. I'm just waiting for the consummate time and place that's all." Sweep it under the carpet!

He quickly changed the subject...a spark of summer. "We're due back the second week after Christmas. Did I mention that the Principal tooth-dragon has halitosis?"

"He was standing next to me one afternoon in the sculpture pen wishing he had such a good rapport with all his other students. I had to retreat from the stench of his issuing firebrand. Then it's on to post-modernism next spring!"

"The rock singer, Sian...she asked me to pose for her book of still-lifes. I wonder what marks she received without me on the front cover? Partly through jejune. That creep Dougal was in! Did you see it? I noticed he didn't hang around long on the night that I *arrived late* to the shag."

"My sister said that you were the nicest girlfriend she'd ever seen me with..."

Warm kisses all the way to the Queen's Hall...Then someone must have read his thoughts. They put that damned record on the jukebox once more!

"It's our song again," he said. "It will always remind me of the bottle party when we held hands underneath the table. They teased us both for being such a pair of lovebirds. Kelvin didn't believe me when I said we hadn't yet. What a face he pulls, really odd, as if it were a crying shame...and he says that you are much too fine for me."

The slave of his erection rose to leave the *lounge* and presumed to walk her to his heart.

"You gave me the idea your parents were rich," she said. "It was rather a disappointment, but it really doesn't matter."

Should he come clean about his antics in the churchyard, and what he did behind the gravestone when he should have been sketching the clocktower?

Would she fall around in stitches if she heard that on that very first day the late starter had carried his house door key gripped tightly in his hand all morning? Should he risk another slap in the face?

'That weekend stay in the Capital, when you hid me in your wardrobe. Farhat the 'Cat' thought the whole fool thing was hilarious.' Kiss and tell.

'But why did you tell me about the Milkman who screwed you in his truck on the way to crammers? Why did you go into details (even when I asked you) about the curtain-raiser when you copulated with your older cousin? The ruffian at the piss-up...was that another opening premiere? And did you have to tell tales out-of-school when befuddled with dipsomania. The *devotee to Iacchus* with the milk bottle in his trousers? And all the rest of them ever since, who have formed a queue from the steps outside the door...leading from your boudoir where you'd wiled the porno books to read. Found in your father's potting shed when you felt the urgent need to *masturbate for England!*'

'Yes! You were filled with false expectations. You were very disgruntled, that time when we were left in peace at the Shambles.' That knocked the cup from your lip. My dear. Into your pile of leaves, Mr. Pogle!

'You said, "Is there anything you want me to do?"
'And I said, "Is there anything you want 'me' to do?"
And the answer to both questions held no brief.

'How could I match up to all of that?'
'Oh! I made plenty of profane excuses! You have to give the devil his due. I'm good at excuses to excuse the *poser* which ached from deep down below.'

'Playing politics with the truth.'
You said, "I thought we were going to make love?"
Make love? Don't make me laugh! Make love? By what means do you expect? How could the *monitor* admit he was just an innocent tourist. While you were...*not a white virgin*...and then 'he' felt 'guilty.'

'I'm good at passing the buck, but perhaps it was just the jitters. All I could think of was to deposit you on the first tram home.'

Just trying to explain a little. My heart had leapt overboard.

'You asked very gently, but I was too proud *ever*...a complete washout.'

'Do you want me to hand you over to the Yardie Mugabe so he can satisfy your unbridled lust from now on?' And Ryan could drive like a demon.

From *Misery Inn* the odd couple dawdled along the row of market stalls from the Penny Arcade along the main street.

At the iron drawbridge of the Castle Gates they parted for the final time below the watchtower of Little Washington.

"I feel a rising coming on!" he fostered. Was he going to levitate? He flinched from her embrace.

The girl with the Germanic glance stamped her heel as she prepared him for the short excursion below the dark wooden chisel. The shadowland of flickering wall gyrated like a row of *origami tigers* above the titles.

"A new velvet jacket just to impress me?" sniffed the chambermaid. "You're shivering blue from cold, never mind the fashionable image! I don't know what to say...I'm very fond of you Mathew darling," purveyed the well-spoken courtesan. "I like your muscles and find you very attractive!" she insisted. "I do not want to hurt your feelings but this is what I sense must come to pass...There's this dishy Italian waiter who keeps giving me the come on. I may not need to get laid but just in case, I think....it would be best for all concerned just to stay good friends. I find that I have to put everything into a relationship, or leave it well alone. Dear Mathew...I'm telling you this for your own good," she cried. "I hope we can still remain in touch. Some people are born to hurt, some to do the hurting."

For the first time in light years he felt unspeakably sad. His heart seemed to grind to a halt, and a lump lodged in his throat. Tried and found wanting was she flinging him out to grass? Should he gallop along after Jennie, and tell her all the things he'd been meaning to say before the *gegenshein became a field of scarlet and black?*

XIX
MIGHTY JO YOUNG

Mary fussed around the *Lodger* as if he were the finest
specimen that had ever trampled across her outer
threshold and entered her domain...

He grunted coursely as he masticated his meal of
roast beef, and when he bent over to lick the plate,
dipping his thick dark sideboards in the residue of
sauce piquante, Mary quite naturally copied his
actions.   Slob-o-dob-o-gobbing-all-over-him!

Tattoed on his forearms was a battleship emblazoned
with the word 'Mavis.' He appeared quite satisfied
with the flunkey. "Oh, I'm so happy," she sobbed.

"Now I can start to 'have a good time!' I've never
been so happy in my entire life," she giggled.

"Isn't the real world wonderful."
Hugging the 'lodger' like a win on the jackpot she
caressed his neck and fondled him suggestively.

"Oh! I'm so happy everyone! Can I have a lick of
your ice-cream cone?" She chuckled salaciously.

Then she proudly bared her clear white teeth which
she always claimed were her most outstanding feature.

One could not deny that her stern despotic glare had
grown less tense now that she was once more in lucre of
a regular supply of 'wild oats,' yet Silcott appeared
far from thrilled and the *purlieus* remained constant.
Avast, buckle-down, all hands on Dick!

"It's a '*business agreement*'," he stressed; they'd
only known each other for a fun packed three weeks
until she popped the question. Alive to opportunity.

The slovernly wench slavering in his earhole had not
mentioned the old hobbledehoy in their prior
negotiations. Shoulder to the wheel son.

"How am I supposed to bring him home with a lout like you still gadding about the house," she scowled.

"Too late to do anything with!" stated the 'lodger' categorically and refused to speak to him directly.

"He's the simplest 'prick' I've ever known," railed the bellicose 'groundworker.' But she had a mind to throw him into science. No relation. Thought they could be pals. Assumed responsibility.

"Where did you find him; the *abortion bucket*?" he asked ridiculously. She sniggered and touched his leg.

"Don't you think I haven't noticed that tribe lurking around outside!" he sneered.

"I've told you where the muttonhead will spend his bottom dollar. Just you mark my bloody words."

"I'm on 'cloud nine,'" she rambled. "I've never felt such a full dinner pail!" Her besotted eyes sparkled as she admired her new engagement ring. "You'd better bugger-off now Mathew," she said. "You've finally run out of rope. The 'lodger' and I will be starting our own family soon, and we don't want you hanging around to spoil the atmosphere or be any part of it. We may be considering adoption, in which case I might eventually have a son to be proud of. And get those stupid weights out of here," she snaked with absolute gusto. "You only eat to compensate!" Was that really so? His mother lolled dreamily over the newcomer's shoulder, teasing and coaxing the former amateur boxing champion to tantalize him further. She draped herself effectuately round his loins and whispered rude words in his ear to see if he would take the hint. The chaste bit of fluff gimmered to share some of their past secrets from the furtive *freak of Nature* opposite.

"If I might mention a rather delicate matter," he stumbled, caught between two stools. "Without meaning to cause offence, but those full-throated troats every single night," he flummoxed. "Could you please be a little more taciturn; it makes me feel uncomfortable."

Well...the schoolteacher gave her 'misfit' son such a *biff*! Mary looked as if she could have killed him on the spot. The lodger tugged on his thick patches of soot and angrily bolted upright.

"If you don't like it you know what you can do," he growled...."Fuck off! You good for nothing little twat."

To pacify her prey the woman continued to smooch with him on the sofa and further embarrass the outsider who was present also.

"Oh! I'm so happy," she wagged, nodding to the stairs, as the 'lodger' bulldozed drearily toward his heap of fulsome hardcore.

She rubbed herself against the anvil of the armchair hose like a 'bitch on heat.'

"Why don't you just sod off!" Mary whispered angrily. "Oh, I haven't done that before," she called after him..."Do I have to tell you everything twice."

"Surely I don't have to pack my bags immediately? There must be some arrangement by which we can go on living with each other amicably. Why do you desire me to vacate the premises so urgently?" Was he kidding?

"So that when you're gone we can screw together on the rug in peace!" grinned the woman....and wandered open-mouthed from the room.

"Is this what you want?" the domestic servant was heard to reitterate down the passage.

She howled even louder than before as the itinerant bedstead hiked bombilatively across the upland prairie.

'It's a knock-out!' Mathew turned the volume switch to maximum on 'World of Sport' to drown the fan-fare bursting along the wharfe.

'How could they dare?' he thought. In broad daylight? A party of girl-guides past by...

The family pet began to howl in synchronized harmony on the top step of the yard. Her devices were proprietously promulgated to the lowest point. Were you born in a field?

What could he say when they returned? How would he dare look his mother in the chops again? Mathew touched his neck like a *Downe's syndrome child*...

Sounds of her rising orgasm screeched into the sunshine as the romping pogo-stick clattered obstreperously against the bathroom complex.

The 'lodger' heavy-laden with animal fertilizer groaned like an *extemporaneous* Bull and shot his load inside the *happy humping heifer.*

§   §   §

With Skippy snapping at her giant heels and leap frogging up her frock she came frolicking down the *Tulip* steps from Holycroft, negotiating the broken bricks, debris, scaffold poles, and timber, peering inside the churning concrete mixer.

"'E lick me all over!" roared Lennie-the-labourer toiling for the brickie on the platform. He mocked her words as if she were an absolute jobbernowl.

"She's even bigger than the wife," he observed. "*Jo-Jo* never be beautiful but just look at those lovely meaty thighs!" he lewdly cooed. The girl arrived to flit around the stanchion.

"Don't you think e's 'andsome Jo' Jo', don't you think he's gorgeous?" Lennie teased the primary school colossus.

"Pretty!" she said. "Just pretty." She shyly hid behind her bushy chestnut mop of hair...

Like a fresh breath of ozone at the rising of the dawn she appeared on the brow of the hill, waving furiously from her parent's four-poster, or bounding boisterously down the winding steps like a graceful young gazelle.

The *Sand-fairy* always chased in hot pursuit to see if she could climb the gate before her. The senior never let *Jo-Jo* out of her sight for long just in case...

Tying knots to the Ethiopean's skin Mathew lured her into the hut when the *orks* had been spread throughout the wide constructions.

The *Sand-fairy* insisted she should be allowed inside the den after submitting the secret password; 'Candyfloss.' Jo-Ho! Hands over ear-lugs...

Sitting tentatively beside the *monitor* with her head confined between her powerful arms *Mighty Jo Young* revealed her sister's teenage crush.

"She dreams about you all night!" she
laughed..."Mathew, Mathew, I've heard her calling in
her sleep"...the *Sand-fairy bitterly* blushed.

But Jo-Jo was the tallest of her kind, and the most
intrinsically eleemosynary.

Her whimsical nature made the giant everyone's
stable companion. She could at this early age already
count the stars.

With her eyes tight shut they played at *pirates and
sailors*, but the *Sand-fairy* could not resist peeping
especially when Mathew sneaked his hand high above the
giant's hem.

His fingers sunk into the plump accomodating
softness of her skin.

Traversing the long bare legs by coign of vantage he
tenderly crept, until he finally made contact...

Suddenly the hut door was sent crashing against the
iron pegs along the rack.

Lennie-the-labourer seethed and quivered in the
doorway as a dust storm spread from the tin lampshade
above them.

He commanded them both to leave instantly. Both
girls turned to water lillies and fled back along the
path to the top of the field.

Then he threatened to inform the *Big Blue Whale* when
he arrived home from the station later that evening.

"I'm ashamed of you Mathew!" he uttered
pretentiously. "We thought you were a decent enough
young lad."

"Promise me that you'll stay away from her in
future. She's a dumb-bell for her age...Don't you
realize that? For two pins I'd have you exposed for
what you've done."

Touched to the quick they steered up the building
site together. He tipped the *melange* of compo into his
hod and tottered up the lower rungs of the ladder.

"He's only jealous because you got to her before he
did," mocked Martin. "You only want to make her bawl!"

"The wife isn't giving him any at the moment so he's
back to the old hand job again!"

His little pecker chipped away at the dry scumble on Inga's bedroom chamber, while his faithful companion loitered patiently on her three front steps, in the bright red boiler suit...

The buxom blonde sloyd flexed her *gargantuan* chest above his balding dome and continued to criticize the Physical Jerk's poor performance in the bedroom.

"He's so out of condition," she sighed. "All *the Naked Civil Servant* wants to do when he gets home from work is go to sleep... why don't you pop around for a coffee when there aren't any more irons in the fire?"

She scrutinized the *grenadier* of the girl who jumped when he opened the door. Jo-Jo had just climbed down a beanpole in the firmament.

"Didn't I see you two in the empty house below the other afternoon?" she smiled. "What were you both doing in there?"

The co-conspirator ignited and stared dolefully into his buds. They made their silent way along a range of empty windows.

At the end of *Greyfriars* crescent the line of poplars swayed and jingled in the pastoral wind, casting a taper, where she leant into a multitude of spirals.

As he cleared the base she presented him with a rocket-lolly from the small concern out of this world.

"I'm so shy," she said. "I'm so very shy!" *Mighty Jo Young* buried herself inside the nearby masonry.

"They tease me at school because of my size," she purled. "I'm an odd bird, but I don't mind," she addled. "I suppose you've heard my nickname..."

As if to demonstrate her preternatural strength the *decajaar* lifted the flaking cement bag above her head in one easy swoop as if she was tossing caber.

She pretended to squint with her left eye in a good-natured rebuke,..."I'll miss you when you're gone!" she said, so incidental and unashamed. There was a fire in her gauze and he waltzed with her head above cloud.

Temporarily choked for a second by this unprovoked comment the corrupting influence hesitated for summer lightning. She rolled back the delay of moisture.

"And I'll miss you too," he sadly replied...

"I'll return for you one day when I've conquered my mountain. Will you bide your time for me?" he asked.

"I couldn't bear the thought of you ever being touched by someone else."

"Don't keep me waiting too long..."
The dormer key slipped smoothly into the clavis lock and 'Mighty Jo Young' ran from the bushes.

For once the leeching skirt of the *Sandfairy* had been given the 'slip.'

She showed him some of the pornographic literature which the local tribe had found drifting around the workmen's *tamping Ark*...one of the specimens hung right down to his knees.

"Aren't we supposed to suck them?" she queried.
"No you certainly are not!" he stared aghast.

"Where did you get such an outrageous idea?"

She knelt in the murky corner as per her instructions while he nervously perlustrated the naked porthole.

Standing on a breezeblock Mathew shifted his gaze to the bollard fastened down the front of his *injured skiffle*.

"Keep your eyes tight shut." he fretted.
He relocated her warmth towards the sharp *metal teeth* and carefully lowered her hand inside his choppermouth.

Her swanlike neck arched over, but her squeamish eyes could not calm, and flickered gently skyward.

"Is that the time?" she squalled.
"I don't know what is to be done..."

He checked the lie of the land again...but something was distinctly amiss.

At any moment Mathew expected the door to fly open and *the watcher* to come bursting inside the refuge.

Suddenly *her* calm demeanour evaporated. A single tear dropped onto the bridge of his hand..."I love you," she sobbed. I'm sure you did.

Mathew bent down and kissed her head.
"People shrink as they grow old!" she said...

Tabatha squatted down on the edge of the housing estate demesne and examined one of the perplexing globules of polystyrene which had been laid in a trail, and which she was collecting fastidiously in the polythene bag which the *bad man* had bestowed.

Out-of-doors she steadily approached from the lip, tossing the shards with fascination in the fanning and brewing them against the summer luminary.

There must have been a *Bank holiday*. It was so quiet they could have been in a ghost town...only 24 hours in a day. Better than collecting tab-ends...

Bird-lime, springled booby-trapped trip-wire.

As the sugar-sweet-shrew approached his snare her tiny bedding-roll was brimming, and her forearms had about as much as they could hold against her lucrative chin. Only a few morsels were left to dart from the plate.

She lapped on the doorway step mesmerized by the evacuee who was waving his favourite truncheon. He had been observing her gradual advance in the full length pane of glass at which he admired himself, resting a couple of yards away against the recent tender.

For eons at one hog she imbibed the solidly erect mass piercing her with its own timeless malice, rubbing her rich brown shoots every so often in case the *iron-gun* had been a *double-vision*.

She reached forward to retrieve the mug sent by Mrs Goldleaf and stroked the velvet surface of his triple cartilage moored on the jetty of his pubic bone, just as the shadow of the Site Agent joined them in happy re-union.

His rapid stride cleared him cleanly to the edge in a matter of milli-seconds.

Grizzled with his fly at half-mast he flew to face the wall and lick his wounds.

"Leave that bobbysoxer alone!" bellowed Paddy O'Brien as Tabatha raced for cover.

XX
FART

Paddy Nutgens 'Fine Art Fairies,' from the bottom of the Polytechnic garden, gathered in the *Buck and Brocket* for their inebriated conference!

Chatter was still circulating about that disgraceful exhibition of 'Performance' Art featuring the gory guillotining on the stage of certain 'vermin,' soon to be mirrored in an actual courtroom case. One of the lecturers involved had just been clapped for forcing a student to drink his urine from a beer glass.

It was the days before the 'Sultans' of Swing' became match-winning, and you could present your 'thesis' in the form of a local 'telephone directory' ('there's the bastard type; now 'you' put it into words!') expecting to achieve a pass with distinction.

Rumours that their guild was soon to hit a blank wall were once again pushed confidently aside, as were the tall stories that Kunst had lost his virginity; an illusion which proved to be totally unfounded.

Little John was absent from the *bacchanalia* after being arrested prancing through the arcade in his pinafore and tutu. The 'singing policeman,' reciting *Under milk wood* in the refectory lift dressed in his birthday suit had been the subject of much heated discussion by the dons of the college scrutinizing his *diction*. A case for the 'happiness police!'

"If you've got it, flaunt it!" cheered Felix Upstart. "A toast to Mammon!"

He still had the remains of his autopsy flaking on his fingers. 666 was autographed on the bridge of his skull. Poser! The *charismatic clone* in the lithe leopard-skin leotard suggested they had a questionnaire to discover if members of their clan masturbated more regularly than other departments in the college. He was the only creature in the known universe who could drink his own weight from a *fountain of human semen*.

His *starting pistol* was certainly original...

This serious inquiry was resolved to some degree by the pale frail little man with balding pate, who was occasionally seen wandering the ghettos in search of greasy combs lying in the gutter, with a flat cap warming the nether cover of his piercing intellect.

The senior tutor contended that students in the second year mistook a seminar for 'half an r.'

"Oh! I think you'd get a reply something like this," he smiled..."Yes! No! Yes! Yes!..No!"

"I believe that in *Egypt* there is an *old wive's tale* it makes men go up the wall."

Then the almighty Nuttall staggered from his trough with a radish in his eye.

He insisted that the need for popularity was a flagrant weakness of his.

The Fat-tub insisted that he deplored the crime of incest although researching his latest blockbuster on 'The Natural History of Fanny-Farts.'

'No man is an island,' he tiraded. 'We can learn far more from you than we ourselves alone can teach.'

He stressed the importance of taking risks and living dangerously, and guaranteed that rules were only there to be broken.

According to Nuttall 'Floaters' in the basin never flushed properly down the drain.

'Some of you cunts only come here to absquatulate in a cave!' he baulked. Wankers of the world unite!

'Do the students consider it more appropriate that they should be trained how to draw properly, or should *painting* be judged by a more subtle form of criteria?'

'Don't we really know the difference between a good pile of shite, and a bad pile of shite?' he frowned.

The *French Nun* was still pestering *Hinchcliffe* to sleep with her in return for a high-enough pass.

"That's a load of shit!" he slurred...and tumbled from his stool.

Said he would rather be digging in the 'Valley of the Kings.'

Had throwing faeces at his audience, then masturbating in front of them, to the annoyance of the *Amazon* women craning over their seats, really been a form of true *Expressionism?*

His 'Sighle na gcioch' dappering the gallery had been admired from every possible angle.

Mathew retired to the bog to attend his fighter pilot's moustache and apply another coat of *Silvikrin*..."Mad enough!" ran his term report...."But I wish he'd get even madder." Once more he returned to the calefaction...

"I wish I'd had praise like that," sobbed Felix..."I knew your sister at Portsmouth. Did you know her sobriquet was penis-breath?"

At the opposite end of the table the enigmatic charlatan glibbed in his scruffy Afghan coat concealed himself behind a pair of dark *watch-lenses*, which glinted oddly under the strip lighting.

Covered by a lengthy funicle of sable he gave a high-pitched girlish titter, not too unlike the intonation of a younker *seamstress*.

"Thought you were a Mr. Supercool when you trotted in the bar with the chick," he tittered. "Everyone here presumed you were one of the big-wigs. I always thought that Vanking was the capital of China myself."

The *medicine-man's* black-and-white pen-and-ink representation of karmic winds entitled 'Osibisa' complemented Mathew's psychedelic watercolours. He had previously been employed as a cabinet-maker whose job it was to measure her body while still warm. Could have been just like the lead singer of *the Faces*.

"Why don't you just shave your head instead of lacquering your strands like corrugated steel?" The art student pushed back his charlike hairline.

"I'm receding too but it doesn't worry me!" he vituperated. Compared to the majority the clockwork mouse picked self-consciously at his pork scratchings. Chip off the old block. Will end up a headcase.

To make matters worse someone played the 'Vinker's song.'

He stared aghast when he realized what was
coming...although the 'difficult one' was impossible he
squirmed like a rubric tom.

"What's the difference between an egg and a bloody
good wank?" asked the enigmatic circumlocutor, his
tinted glasses glaring queerly in the harsh overhead
illumination. The cast cogitated a second.

"You can beat an egg," he maundered.
"What are you then?" queried the *pongye*.

"I'm a green manalishi with a three-pronged prong!"
spurted Bates in thunderous response, straightening his
fractured spectacles mended with a piece of elastoplast
by an adept cross of his cranking utensil.

"Why don't fairies get pregnant?" he
asked..."Because they only go to *goblin* parties!
What's green and smells horrible? Answer...a boy
scout!"

"Did you hear the one about the nun?...got
excommunicated for doing press-ups in the carrot
field!" he reitterated.

Bates had recently tried to *hang himself* from the
studio balcony as a *sacrifice to Old Gooseberry*. The
stunt had backfired by the time they cut him down
almost comatose.

A docket underscored his tidemarked neckline.
'Always flow with the stream,' he whinged.

He swore that there was no such thing as an exactly
straight line although he had spent many years trying
to find one.

"I hear that you do *Pumping Iron*? Doesn't he look
sweet when he blushes," he chuckled. "Is that really
mascara festooned round your eyes?"

There was an invitation to the echo chamber but
Bates dampened the idea with another dram.

He'd once seen a billboard saying 'Drink Canada dry'
and he was determined to make an attempt before the
finish. On the turbulent crossing to Amsterdam he had
been the only one left standing in the bar.

"The only musical instrument I've ever played was a
'barley-sugar whistle' which I found in a lucky bag,"
he hissed.

After a break for last orders Felix drew attention to
the horde of entartetes.

"Has anyone seen those graven images buried on the
ninth floor...similar to the flour-faced *Bedlamites*
chained with spiked collars in prismed coffins?"

The queer cartoons tucked at the back of the drawer
caricatured masculine clowns with hideous hook noses
and protuberating lips engaged in fellatio and buggery
on an acrobat's swing. S + M.

Their glance fell towards *the Nixy* who had
hypnotized their heed. Had once been a Cellarman at
the Widow's Revenge.

It was the age of punk when Charlie Wax could
compose with a melted candle horribly deforming one
side of his face spitting like a 'wonder dog'...even
Nigel Bates trick with the Vesta's couldn't put a spark
into him. There was definitely something fishy about
his whole art of the possible.

"Look at that!" he slurred, rancorously pilastering
his 'pregnant' gut; "And I never eat anything! All I
want is to photograph beautiful chicks so I can fuck
with them afterwards!"

A *pin-snapper with Mohican spikes* arrived in the bar
through the saloon door wearing a T-shirt bearing the
logo 'The Police are Coming!' in black capitals
emblazzoned across her bouncing young mammaries.

"I hope someone cleans up the mess afterwards!" he
sniggered.

"This is how to do it!" he sneered in a mocking
'Punch and Judy' chant.

Bates continued to empty the magic matchbox
theatrically on the top so that he was not spoiled for
choice. The girls all turned their heads away in
disgust. Get Knotted!

"I used to be into *necrophilia* until some rotten
cunt split on me," he whimpered disagreably.

He struck a match on the side of the tinder
sandpaper to illustrate the illusion reached through
long drunken hours of cogitation.

With a simultaneous flick of his wrist the enigmatic Bates impaled the burning stalk quickly into the soft and tender crutch of his butchered palm, and gave a fake little groan as he pressed the weapon home.

His smouldering flesh blistered afresh and his skin quivered and cracked with a new scar gleaming among the old.

"*Ragamuffin!*" he cackled with delight as he held his arm politically in the air to demonstrate his foul allegiance.

"Everybody look at me!" he bantered...as the cemented matchstick stabilized in mid air without any support at all. Was he going to call for a bucket? Why weren't some of the leading Statesmen and women Black magic Saucerers? Then!

The sore red palm griped with the blackened end of the wood as Bates urgently screamed for another prong to see how many could be stood on board. Sit on your hands and keep buttoned-up.

Perlustrating this bizarre spectacle the Billiard-Ball with the worn-out skirt of back mustered from the distant *Cairn-group*. The *cider-makers* were obviously perfect candidates for his recruitment drive.

His white dome glaring beneath the lamplight 'Wig' propositioned them with one eye on the exceptional.

"I've just had a brain-wave!" he enthused. "Some of us want to form a 'Fine Art' society in the college to discuss points of mutual interest...do any of you want to join?"

"And what do you propose to call this band of piss-artists?" boomed the strummer. Said he was into selling pharmaceuticals.

"Why not call your group *Fart*?" suggested Bates...their rhetoric bucked like a rollercoaster!

They vacated the empty vaudeville after closing just as the three Nags were starting away on the pavement, and in a moment of rare spontaneity decided to shadow them in the hope of breaking their duck. A natural calamity had stunted his arrested development.

"Trust me!" Bates voice boomed from the bottom of a well.

Like an *alternating current* the three Boggarts dressed in buckskins tracked the girls as if their whole future depended upon the outcome.

The cackling of broody hens made Nigel Bates feel quite respectable as they footstepped over caravans in the snow...

A marathon pool session that day had resulted in a disorderly quarrel at the summit of their game. The pool-shark had caleered the loser with disasterous results. But it still wasn't worth breaking all his fingers.

The cue had been suddenly hurled in his direction. His spectacles had been trampled on the ground as he scythed on his hands and knees.

Instead of retaliating against his opponent the contestant had kicked the blockage at the exit with such force that his foot had become rooted in the timber panel...

As they trolled along the avenue Mathew could not help noticing that Bates was not wearing any buskins...the hole which blossomed at the pole of his carpet slippers was now exposing his niggardly big-toe.

"I can hardly walk now!" he complained braggardly, as the sickening pincer, like an enormous lump of jet, set like serried ranks amid the sharp December fall, spreading its poison from the base of his shaft.

"I always wanted to be a tramp when I grew up!" he grinned.

"Where are we going?" It was a hopeless, hopeful situation...in time a limited conversation developed between the drips.

"There's gonna be a *ripping*!" Bates tactfully blurted...the girls began to get a sharp move on again!

"Why don't you ask them if they're married?" asked Felix in his light fingered dialect. "I never try anything with someone I really like..."

"Look, stop *projecting* your sentiments onto me!" ranted Bates, and began his old ramble repeating himself.

"Why do I keep on repeating myself?" he asked them, seriously at first. "Why do I keep-on fucking repeating myself?" he wrangled...on, and on forever.

An iron bar down the front of his forehead would have met requirements...

From afar they carefully marked the number of the terraced slum where the trio had imported.

After loitering outside their headquarters for an hour they were miraculously invited in for a late night cup of coffee after rapping on the knocker.

Explaining their wyrd antics was a piece-of-piss. They arranged to meet them the following evening in a more conventional setting. Apparently it wasn't even their own accomodation. Another trick up his sleeves.

Bates raged that deodorants were enviromentally repugnant.

After only twenty minutes the three stooges were once more summarily ejected into the cold damp street from where they came just as Bates was repeating the joke about *convent practices*, with the seven mile intercurrence to make home again.

"I'm sorry lads but some of us have to get up in the morning," she glared and slammed the door. "Bog off!"

Bates was furious after this short respite, and paralysis was edging up his bare calf towards his thinking cap.

"I'm not going to be taken to the cleaners!" he persisted in vile distress. "Don't give firewater to the fucking Indians! Wogmeat!" He chastised the brass plate of her cribble and screamed through the radiating letterbox.

Then, giving his two fingered victory salute, Bates viciously thrust the said two fingers down his defecating throat...not so easy!

A spurt of vomit erupted out of his mouth and obliterated the number plate. A treacle of gunge trudged down to the embossed bleb of the door wart. There was definitely something of the Grand-Bel in Nigel Bates.

"Excellent!" he choked, and staggered off down the lane....

Is there life on *Mars?* Pseudo-logique extraordinaire.
How are you celebrating your twenty-first?

Long after the kitchen clock had struck midnight the
vagrant lodger sneaked surreptitiously up the stairs
with the mechanism still clanking loudly in his
eardrums.

In the object red brick Victorian astragal the
vestibule pale was slightly open...a glimmer of
phosphor spangled from the sarkstone as he crept by
their four poster chamber.

'He hadn't touched her for years,' she moaned into
his taffeta phrases.

The Boarder ambled past the Snoopy door toward the
sink and scouted for the invitation card which she must
have forgotten to post.

"Oh! you have got a 'dirty' mind!" The doubtful
anguish had died away since their recent *diamond
jubilee* though. Thought he could hear a hoot.

With a backward glance he noted the bar of light
below their casement suddenly vanish.

The Post-Graduate Medical students living above had
enjoyed another brilliant copulation, so all was quiet
on the Western front...

Our *Boarder* set about arranging his gear, but no
matter how much he vexed, he simply could not decide on
a suitable attire...

Should he dress himself in the pair of pink
slippers, or slip into the nightie the gammer had
granted?

The knickers printed with 'Half-Way Inn!,' or simply
go in the all-together.

From pit to empyrean he fretted and held them both up
to the moonlight.

With no greater love than this he closed his closet
door, and approached the 'Snoopy' place cautiously at
first. What a stroke of luck it had been right next
door to his!

Carping his slobber to the paintwork his stethoscope
went on red alert. White noise!

"Come out little 'piggy,' where ever you are" he sibilated. Whirling like a dervish he held one hand over his eyes and pointed with his finger like a Searcher.

His insatiable appetite homed in on her delicious purring. Was it here the comical spectacle became unending farce? He suppressed a sanguine howl with his hands full of jockey.

Just when you weren't expecting such temerity Grendel 'Nosferatil' had to make his presence felt.

The squeaking pivot slowly anchored, and he shuffled his devious way inside with the kegs taut around his scamping ankles.

With a rising flood of blood Grendel tossed the scrap of garlic hanging above the portal in the trashcan.

To a flourish of inner trumpets he danced a swift lambada and examined her with his torchlight flush against her maroon lips.

He frollicked confidently with her frock folded on the buffet, snooping omniverously through her underclothes and garments. With a queer contempt he protested the impotent artifacts languishing round the dingle and standing guard in the roundhouse of the feeble atalaya.

His unmistakable imprint posed in the perspex of the built-in wardrobe as the fatted calf snoozed on her golden rug.

Cuddly toys and bric-a-brac, the aggravating Snoopy clock, manuscripts, hieroglyphs, and even a Snoopy duvet, failed to keep the ghoul in check, but simply made him feel over the moon.

He knocked the largest Snoopy dog from his wicker turret and declaimed at the crossroads that he should ever be inhibited by such tame canine ikons.

Grendel trod deeply into the soft shag pile. He skulked furtively by the leaded orifice until his filthy habit could be satisfied with fresh blood.

Hug-and-mugging in cloak-and-dagger he prowled through a veil of natural shroud. The floodlights of the stadium had been dimmed...thank god!

73

In the *White room* Tiffany turned her darling head, and rebuked the monster with her sighs for having been delayed.

As if by common consent the pretty young petal stared toward her fluctuating nocturne...the manic beamed delightedly with aspirin looks of happiness.

With his rude awakening weighing into the eiderdown he replaced the loose held diabalo which had fallen insolently from her grasp to rest more securely snuggled at her side.

With tender loving care the *unhallowed spirit* mocked the presence of the flies and adroitly manoeuvered the supple hand conveniently hanging over the edge of her haven to wax-and-wane on his wavering snakehead...but the nimble digits rapidly absolved and recoiled to hug around her 'more' accustomed endearment.

In a fit of rage he cursed and spat. How much longer till he got the damned thing straight? He fiddled with the balance of her differing shoulderblades.

Eventually Tiffany seemed to sense just what the doctor ordered; she wriggled to rest dead centre with her lucrative gallypot drooping dreamily ajar exactly on the verge of the quilt...

Quivering with suspense his seething fangs clappered like a night hawk. A black raven landed on the drain to crow outside the falstaff.

Tossing back the superfluous material he removed the grossly impeding plug from her desire-able griker and laid it gently over her robot pillion.

The mist of his mien crawled over the bones like a tarantula.

He manoeuvered his 'tower of Babel' to align with her dread.

With true dexterity, and almost double-jointed, he lowered the beast necessarily towards the gurgling enterprise....pressing tight against her soft wet gums desiring the fragrance of her kiss.

At long last she recited the correct liturgy.

Shaded dark by moonlight with his misty vision cleared
he churned the unremitting labours of his love and
jarred against the rigid pearls of her sparkling
molars.

With his knee buttressing against her headboard the
tiny virgin semblance clenched and unclenched her
trapped and griping palm. With the tonne of his maw-
worm fagging his pounding heart he forced the hazard
stream to scale the heights of sophomore. He urged the
pouting mushroom to release the pressure building in
his toggle. Great balls of fire. A whitewash.

With his straining pick-a-back becoming numb *Grendel*
uttered the magic words; 'Open Sesame!'

But the incantation whispered so despairingly was
without its final charm, and this was no Arabian night.

Her free hand reached up to grip his stem
mechanically in her parchment.

Grubbling her taste-buds over their glittering grid,
where a glob of syrup wheedled its viscous path into
her swallow-hole, sweet Tiffany's eyes opened right on
schedule. She issued the penultimate command tickling
an eyelash on Old Lugger creamed in saliva.

Her eyebrows considerably narrowed as the tingling
sensation began to reach *boiling point*, and the pumping
began like an explosion down the *mineshaft*, filling her
gaping gap with the best of his life-kindling juices,
which splashed so abundantly over cheek and jowl.

Remnants of the guzzling flocked her feather pillow
as he quickly faded out of sight and lost himself among
the slobland.

From the nadir of her robes the prowling fiend
counted his blessings as sweet Tiffany sat bolt upright
in her shorties. She touched her creamy skin where the
ambrosia still dripped like molten sugar and began to
cough and splutter insults.

Grendel trembled beneath the cliff of the
escarpment.

Peering out of focus her hazy indignation snorted a
hum of exasperation towards the crouching bundle before
settling down once more to slumberland...

But the voyager had not yet reached his final port of call; 'Nosferatil' wandered by the silken shards and admired the portrait of her recent atavist. He examined each intimate belonging before deciding with which close encounter he would like to convene his nuptuals.

The imminent pitch of dawn would still find him tending lovingly to her crinal curtains with the 'Snoopy' comb....the troublesome Snoopy alarm would still be waving its luminous limbs from the mantelpiece.

Before she mounted the scaffolding he would be chased away by the breaking of the 'making' spell.

The cat-burgular gave a disgruntled 'tut' 'tut' as he envisaged how he would respectfully remit the white door after his departure...

Mrs. Do-as-you-would-be-done-by, panting pathetically at his valance, would gently knock on his latch in the early morning streak.

If she was fortunate the old dutch might gain a peep of his hard-on; but only if he forgot to put on the bolt and pulled down his sheets like the best of all people.

A shiver ran down the Sleep-walker's spine as he wondered how long the debauched love affair could continue nose to tail. He stalled like an alabaster corpse...

Could no-one drive a merciful stake through his heart, and convert this shame to sadness?...and say, "Come on h-o-m-e, Mathew, all is forgiven!"

XXI
BALD EAGLE

The Golden Sunflowers brought tears of joy whenever
Mathew flashed across their vibratile seed of colour...

After visiting the 'Outsider's' exhibition at the
Hayward the Farters retired to the 'Elephant and
Castle' for pie and peas.

Otto Baldung had received a split lip after
attempting to ruffle his tattered plumage. The
corrugated steel shell of the tortoise was like a
motley bed of rags.

A senior lecturer languished in a nearby jail
charged with G.B.H. after attacking a bus conductor
with a bowl of jelly...

The *barley haired Germanic beauty* nudged her best
friend with her elbow.

'Who was the jerk with the rippling biceps?'
Mistook for 'Wings.'

His jerkin buttons seemed to disintegrate with ever
higher levels of intoxication....

Ulrike was the apple of every young blade's eye.
Even Nigel Bates laid claim that it was him who she
stared so longingly towards.

Tented in her *perfect oscillations* the sensitive
Renaissance features added enchantment to her comely
Streepian smile.

How he longed to run his slippery fingers through
those gilded waves...

It was difficult to decide which were the more
beautiful. Should he gently brush her aureate curls.

She puzzled over small beer. He just resisted the
temptation to scorch his hand. The stray nipple
glimpsed in the exam.

When Gollum returned from the thunderbox he appeared
absolutely radiant. His most recent procurement was
still combing her straggly matted locks.

Earlier in the week he had been on show strutting his wares in a male talent contest organized by *Calendar*. But it had turned into a big flop.

If he opened his mouth he could shatter goblets. "A right Jack-the-lad," Bates observed.

Spying the comb-collector surveying the 'Stocks and shares' he immediately commented that 'Ram Elevators' were on the 'up!'

Brandishing recent conquest so smugly on his face Gollum tackled Mathew on surely his weakest point to date. A perfect ten!

"You! *Bald Eagle*," he hollered across the foyer..."When did you last have a wank you ugly-bald-headed-*bastard?*"

His target postphoned publishing the highest testosterone count in the city. Turned him into a 'smoothie' in the first place. The groupie turned her chair away. Let some air get to it!

Spread-eagled in the middle of the company Gollum began to discuss Mathew's ruling passion with the assembly of carvers.

He stirred the group into another turbulent palaver. 'Rather snog the bell-ringer's hump?!'

Disguised in the darkened bar the kook frollicked to some obscure reggae rhythms...

Bates reckoned he must have descended from the Red Planet.

"Old Baldy must keep *Silvercream* in business!" A few scarlet faces struggled desperately to channel their energies into a more productive outlet.

Peculiar emissions erupted from the area of their gullet, hands were rushed to cover up the embarrassment, and tears prickled with dust in the filament.

There was something of the 'Ryan Starbuck!' Fruity. Gollum fanned the field of keeling wheat with another tickling wind...put a screw on it.

Cram down the throat. Put a lid on your escapement.

He briefly acknowledged their thin end of the wedge
with a half puzzled smile, vaguely discerning perhaps
that he himself was the but of the knitting bee?

The music-master nonchalently persisted to strike
chords as beads of sweat glistened down the fine mousey
strands flying up his dinner jacket. Rachmaninov's
concerto in C minor. His glance flew round the walls
of the music-room.

Blotches of *mess-mother* appeared on Nigel Bates
corpulent curried neck as he capsized into a number of
odd contortions.

Cantillating like castrati he stumbled stupefied
through the recess, and threw himself into a *Van Dyke*
melancholia.

'Ghandi's revenge' he said. Couldn't make head nor
tail of it...

Felix had carried a haunted look ever since the first
blush of new term. He had spirited himself away to the
upper storey in an effort to muddle through the
anaglyph of plastic arts.

He pensively eschewed the wibble-wabble of the
rhythm method and gleamed skywards.

As he placed an X in the polling booth the Brummie
born and breed was approached by the first year.

The newcomer bellowed like a foghorn...his wrists
were still dangling in swab.

"Don't do it!" he grumbled blearily. "It's not high
enough!"

This unhinged minder-of-metal with the implacable
gesticulations of a fascist dictator had engineered a
tool-pattern of clods to be plied into operation,
carefully measured and announced, crammed with ever so
many mechanical devices, assembled in the gasification
plant of a distillery. Pinnochio had vanished once or
was it twice before..."Do you think he could be round
the twist?" wondered Bernice.

He demanded to know whether she swallowed or spat.
Palleted away on the stretcher he screamed *undying love*
for the girl he'd never met before, having already had
his wooden stems chopped across the kerbstone by a
lynching mob...

The oddball piece of blacklegging, uncannily resembling
the reproductive images in his plans, pulled a sequence
of harrowing expressions as he caught the 'life-class'
in progress. He made several oblique references about
his arms being roughly proportionate to the size of his
penis. Needed a knee capping.

"Play the white man you thick black bastard!" he
farted.

"The way I look, is because of the way I look!" he
prattled. Bates instantly acclimatized with him. The
blood-donor brimming with Prince Alberts looked about
to land a blow. He was still wearing that liver-
stained blue jersey set like iron over a month ago.
Didn't give a monkeys. Only a harmless jape.

"Well, I've gone and done it at last!" sniffed Felix
with a sense of doom and blithe despondency. He wiped
the tears from his eyes.

"I just couldn't put it off any longer."
They both sympathized with his predicament, but even
Bates had an eagle in his stomach.

Felix nodded sagely and dragged the skeleton clear
from his wardrobe.

"You screwed her then!" gleamed the drawing-pin
eater...

"Old fat *Bessie the black labrador bitch?*"
"Yes!" he confessed '*diis aliter visum.*' "And I enjoyed
every minute of it!" He piped.

Duelled over pork scratchings.
"Who's been writing wisecracks all over my bedroom
wall?"

'Still having those nightmares Gollum? When did you
last smash up your shack in a frenzy of slumber?'

Bates swore blind he was a madman when he was
pissed.While the craps away!

The exhibitionist in stars and stripes glared at
Bates for letting the cat out of the bag.

"Bit of a touchy character yon, isn't he?" insinuated
Gollum.

"What if he were a *latent homosexual and educationally subnormal?*"

"You will be!" interjected Bates icily...
"Will be what?"

"*Sorry!*" he drilled and grinned. "Have you got a cough?" asked Bates facetiously, and chaffed his itching testicles.

"No he couldn't be!" laughed Gollum shaking his head.

"Besides, he told me already that he was still a little virgin, and has never had a steady girlfriend!"

Linked to the phases of the Moon the invisible assailant carried his artful dodger piggy-back through the University campus towards the distant Zeppelin. It was All Souls.

Placing a pair of milk-bottle tops over his eyes he pretended to stumble around in the dark clutching a white cane. "I'm blind as a Blunkett tonight," he chortled. "How old are you anyway?" he asked.

"I was begotten on the banks of the *River Tigris* over five thousand years ago," he echoed. "There, or there abouts." The surly Bates proclaimed to the Big Dipper. "I challenge all the *bugbears* in creation to overwhelm this bird of prey," he blared.

'Similar invocations were not always consummated immediately,' he declared.

After a showdown at the *amusement arcade* Mathew landed at the digs for a special treat. He flicked through the family snapshots with Tiffany fidgeting nervously from the nearby escarpment. He yawned. His brain was fagged. Every hag needs her...

"And this is when we enjoyed a short spell in *Transylvania*," she beamed.

"We were so happy in those days: I don't know why we ever left the forest."

"Can I ask you something in private?" she asked. "Do you always believe in bloodsuckers?"

"Why do you wish to know?" he said studying her *grike.*

"One autumn festival I was in my room fast asleep when I woke up to find an enormous shape hovering above me..."

"My dad said, 'it'll be him!' What do you think it could have been?" She shuffled her feet and prepared to draw her own conclusions. Flagrant abuse of power and privilege.

Could have called for the batmobile.
The lodger was polaxed for a second. His lips turned chalk white. Sitting on pins-and-needles.

"Perhaps it was the specter of your recently departed, dear old grandfather?" he answered.

Mathew belvedered for signs of open rebellion...he scrawled 'Wangled' across her maths homework.

On the jaded road below traffic flowed like a mysterious mutant army as he turned his head for what he vowed would have to be the penultimate injection of the radio-active wonder serum.

His bloodshot eyes rolled towards the roast insensible of all consequence on the banquetting cloth as he removed his bleeding biretta.

A flock of inquiring sycamore fell from the russet eaves above and floated by the window of the White room as the stealthy steganographer admired the X-ray photograph by the ebbing phosphor of Selene's silver lamp.

Like a repugnant gargoyle he flew in a flailing motion over to her bedevilled frame. The glitter of his discordant image appeared from the grey of his separate double life.

With a sickly grin spreading beneath the unturfed thatch from ear to ear he contemplated the tender excesses of his composition and began ringing the chimes of the 'Moonlight sonata Interfada.'

"You will!" he stated with expert venom. "You must!" he warned her vehemently with extra tocsin.

The single entity perching desolately on her naked reef prepared to meet the perspiring late night stalker shivering catastrophically.

His hand slid beneath the garb towards her unpledged hiney like a mole.

"Why did you?" he asked her..."Why did you?" he sibilated. "Who in heaven's name gave you permission to place a chair behind your virgin white ingress?"

But he would not be baulked, should not be baulked! The buffer had been gradually displaced to the doppelganger's delight.

'Nosferatum' gnashed his flints of calcite and snapped an eye from the crummy Snoopy boss....

With his bald dome bowed the silhouette placed two fingers over the twin small pikes, and pegged them together with a pinch of his lank fulvous nails.

Immediately Tiffany's mouth abruptly distended. He skreaked with elysium at having discovered how to settle old scores.

With his hook nose bent the journeyman explored the deepness of the tomb, where his brain-child's body supined in suspended animation.

To bay the moon he placed the ashdown thermometer in her hand...but the renegade quickly withdrew.

When he returned with greater force she gnawed the ridgelike waterway with her pins and her hand trickled down the rising stem... gummies!

In the amanuensis of the looking glass Grendel perlustrated his crowning glory, pressing the crooked spear into her quest of iron...illustrious crammer!

Suddenly Tiffany stirred, perhaps offended by his omnipotent position, and refused to take the sacred unction offered as a laxative.

Her contraceptive grip educated down the flinching tool to savour the flavour of his pubic region.

Nosferatum froze like acid marble as the pupil searched beneath his dripping testicles and held the hirsute bollocks stiffly in her cooler hands.

"Get stuffed, Bald Eagle!" she fathomed faintly, as if she were hailing from the bottom of some ancient Celtic ink-horn.

What a way to speak to her crammer. He mumbled the lord's prayer backwards and wailed 'Fool's mate!'

"For God's sake leave me in the Land of Nod," she
hissed with loathing.

"But...but I'm a doctor!" he stuttered. "You've
forgotten to take all your buttercup syrup."

The bungler flew like a bald bat out of hell back to
the secret recesses of his unhallowed pit and fell into
a melting mood. He shivered as if his useless
existence was finished, breaking out into a cold
unhealthy downpouring.

It looked as if he was floating in it. It was a dirty
bird indeed that fouled its own nest.

Was this to be the culmination of 'Nosferatil's'
cankered esse? He would surely be tried with a
sanctified stake through his palpitating core, and
final, unexpurgated *euthanasia.*

Head-hunters crunking in the *pantry,* entering their
chamber through the trap-door, she stormed, panic
stations, vain regret!

The irate *villagers* were gathering under the gloomy
shadows of the bell tower...shambling behind the
barrier reef..milkies!

Lanterns and shadows squiggled the dark-door as the
alert stockman pursued the passageway for the evil
manifestation.

A clarion call of yoiks oscillated through the
entire house and into the dove-cote as he *copied a dead
man* with the iron bolt carefully drawn.

Anybody there? Thunders of the Vatican! Her father
examined the floor for a *poltergeist* disturbance but
still they omitted to vex his dampened bridge.

Crazy as a garbage collector. Six feet under. Sold
out of commission.

"Go back to bed!" the forces Chaplain pragmatically
recommended. "Ghosts can't hurt you, only the living
will!" Sleep safe my tortured love...

At the first cockcrow of dawn the morning blush of
sunlight found his webbed feet hopping rapidly over
pales.

XXII
THE CARROT MUNCHERS

The pale-face in the flag-room often seemed to be suffering from *jet-lag* as the Soap floundered like a dumb waiter on the screen.

From the lofty rear window passing shoppers could be observed flitting through the streets like distant ants.

Across the arcade the bimbo strained towards the booby-hatch of kinetic mummy-cloth.

Sairy Gamp peered round the corner of the door to check if he had swallowed all his pills.

She glanced in his *secret file* lying open on the vestibule, complete with its dossier of sappy snapshots.

'*Needs Heavy Sedation!*' was stapled to the front cover.

The special nurse congratulated him on his commitment to stay with the company at their never to be repeated reduced rates.

In the proneos of the amphitheatre she craned over his loss of condition with the flashbulb.

The distinguished quack had dodged in to the light opera. His name and titles over the door were practically obliterated with spiderwebs.

"From here?" she smiled, hesitating with the red felt pen above his bald spot...Mathew trembled on the edge of his swivel.

"Forward a bit more," he haggled. "I have a birth scar on my bonce which used to be hidden, and I would like it to do so again, if possible."

Before the *superficial* digging of his turf could proceed...

"Replanted roots will not take on broken tissue, but we'll do our very best, although I think the crown is in a much worse state of repair than your receding forehead!" Full marks for observation then. Boodle and broke. She called a spade a spade.

Once the operator had marked out the *receiver site* they shaved a rectangle the size of a cassette, which would be used as the *donor area*, from the back of his memory device.

"We'll soon give you a 'head of hair' you can be proud of, cure you of this wretched illness and boost your flagging confidence. The holes in your scalp will shrink to the very tiniest dots on a cheese grater and become practically invisible to the naked eye."

He was helped to his feet and led swaying dizzily into the torture chamber. The Video was immediately plugged-in to divert his driving attention.

As they disregarded 'Rainbow' numerous injections from the steel spike were administered into both territories with local anisthetic. Cloud cuckoo land. Off 'his' bleeding rocker!

Before he could squeal the drill began to collect its hirsute cargo, sending circulation fluid spurting from the mincing blades cascading down his neck.

Each tiny disc bore between one and eight hair follicles it was alleged. A fact!

Prattling deliriously twenty to the dozen the macho man turned for them to calm his fevered grasp.

He postured in the armchair as if he was travelling backwards on the Corkscrew ride. Close your eyes.

Though it was directly against orders the girls offered him their *Lambert and Butler* which he chain-smoked throughout the entirely natural ordeal.

"I never liked Mr. Spore the dentist either," he trembled. "I would do anything to avoid his company on the way home from my lessons!"

Eventually the head case was in such a state that Mr. Marshall, the salesman with the pointed pencil moustache, and even the *concerned director*, were dragged in to stand warily by his side.

The only thing he had in common with E.T. was his lack of consistency.

That famous inventor of the *terrific-trefine* and all the rest of the management team were gathered in the pits calling out slap-happy encouragement.

His condensation interfered with their mechanical gadgets.

Over half a century of plugs were transported from one *bomb site* and stapled deliberately in another, while 'St. Joan' kept rabbiting on about her stay with the *Mad Brushman of Seville*.

The sharp fast teeth of the *carrot munching machine* gnawed into his flesh like a rat hungry rabbit.

Its mouth spat out the provisions like *buckshot* onto the *billiard ball* sweating profusely from all directions.

He turned slightly and caught the belligerent eyes of the director, who immediately warmed and passed this crumb of comfort...

"I hope you don't presume that this will make you good looking or alter your success with women," he advised, expiring to leave the room. "Some of our patients come here under the false impression that a hair transplant will suddenly make them attractive to the opposite sex...!" He laughed and rubbed both his hands together. All the way to the bank sir if you please!-a doctor, a medicine-man.

"All I want is a roof over my head!" sniffed the 'flying Dutchman' in his punishment chair, filled with preposterously high expectations.

The headcase continued to explain the hidden complexities of 'Mentalism' to his audience, discussing the 'meaning of life' with the creasing bloodsuckers.

"But I believe our true purpose is simply pro-creation!" he suggested; the inventor seemed quite confident he knew what he was talking about.

Mathew paid a fast buck for this jump from the frying-pan. No six inch sutures at this juncture. No scrubbing away the scabs before time on this *six month cycle of a thousand cuts*.

Cold steel needles tunnelled under his stuff, as the fosser munched through the back of his wide open *water-melon*. With lymph glands juicing he stared fearfully into space like an automoton with paranoid eyes.

"Not long now!" she chortled merrily. "We're nearly done!"

"You'll soon be able to go home to your wife, but remember, *no sex for three whole days!* The grafts need a short period to re-settle. Do not wash your new hair for at least a fortnight."

She mopped the channel as his heartbeat pounded, and the red-hot lava trickled into his thought processes.

Suddenly there was a bright flash above the performance; the electric lightbulb had burst. The stuttering arc showered its glassy cartilage through the eclectic atmosphere, to explode on the giant base.

Both their lumpers looked stunned..."Oh! Golly," she gasped. "That's never happened before." She rushed to catch the salesman who was loitering in his newspaper.

But the proceedings were soon brought to a speedy conclusion.

Mathew was helped out of his drubbing for the *Great Dane* to swap places in the former *abbatoir*.

The surgical dressing wrapped tightly round his head added vertigo, and a sudden nausia welled up in his abdomen as he observed himself in the Gentleman's looking-glass carrying the flag.

The *numbskull* peered at his pale and ashen face and rubbed his mole-coloured sockets...he'd certainly aged five years during the four hour operating process, and yes, there was a white hair already avoiding his restricted circulation bodice.

"See you soon I hope!" she gleamed obligingly. "Reception has just advised me that your wife is here to collect you! If you encounter any problems please give our recorder a buzz..."

The lift plummeted to the ground floor where the woman waited on the thoroughfare beside the outer springboard.

Through the iron girders of the *locust* cage he glimpsed her etiolate spectre. Lump-shit...

He emerged into a grim and woeful daylight swaddled like the 'Phantom of the Pharaoh's Opera.'

The teacher cudgelled his arm as he tottered wearily over the cobbles. His swollen turnip-head throbbed like a football as he groped his way along the wall.

Familiar market dwellers stopped to pillory him as the gowk struggled to stretch the *tea-cosey* over his outpouring clock...

"Oh! Mathew, well done!" she clapped.   "At last you've had some decent 'common' sense. But it was all your own fault really. I always told you not to go on those awful sunbeds...You are a pain in the neck. If it hadn't been this it would have been something else," she warranted...Somebody left the door open, and the wrong dog came home.

The chump awoke from the recurring vision which suborned him to return to that radioactive dungeon with a ringing in his ears. Dabs of dried fop still lingered to the stained night pillow, and he could hear his mother's call startling up the stairs.

"Come on down Mathew!" she moaned. "Look who's here to see you." Their pedal bikes were moored beneath the sunfilled foliage.

Withdrawing hastily under his tent Mathew flagged-down his wiry raddled nose-beard.

He tapped tentatively on the paintwork. His best friend paced up and down beside the grill.

"Don't you understand that you can't possibly emulate my honours of battle," he chuckled.

Ryan Starbuck rotated his round blue peeps and made them go all cross-eyed.

Mathew's solitary eyes peered out from the spunk-hole. He slowly emerged like a shy wrinkled hermit. Gone deaf as a post. Nerves slashed. Couldn't fuck.

"The diving club all want to know where you have disappeared. I've brought Stephanie along to see you. We want you to be best man when we tie the knot in spring."

Mary led the *sun-tanned Aphrodite* to where the invalid immediately faded once more into his bundle of parchment. How now my fine feathered friend.

His hand wound like a thread-worm from the darkness. "My mother is so looking forward to meeting your acquaintance. She had an accident in the schoolyard on Wednesday while on dinner duty..."

"It was so windy that her hair-piece blew off and all the children were in hysterics while she chased it round the yard."

The *toxic warrior* materialized for a restorative draught of skim. No cannibals or Milesian women.

"We think it's the best thing that you've ever done," they agreed. He reared his ugly T-bag steak.

To his surprise Ryan Starbuck bent over and kissed him on the head...."That does it!" laughed his fiance.

"I always thought there was something going on between you two..."

His spire had been ravaged with fire and sword. Head like a plastic dolls.

Mathew stubbornly rocked his bloater. Daft as a brush. Mad as a fucking hatter.

"I'm definitely not going to put in the kitty until this is all over," he pledged.

"That is going to be the last time anyone calls me *Bald Eagle!*"

*   *   *

He tramped to the bottom of the trichonosis and glanced sharply behind him.

All that the monstrous birth perlustrated were the creepers entwined in the branches scaffolding the flazen gable.

Crossing up the frozen stairs of concrete he emerged into the plateau's baking summer heat wearing only his blue jeans, except for that ridiculous batch of wool the plasterers were always attempting to eviscerate.

In the mansion across the *boulevard* that *damned loose-liver* lingered in her menagerie of felines.

At their garden gate the *innocents* were entering with a *bag of rice.*

Dirty Harry stumbled like a Boston Strangler. After karaoke night at the Beacon his artificial cogs had been puked down the lavatory.

The hairy little gnome with the *garde-l-o-o-ed* glass bauble fretted over his vagrant sleep-walking.

He was convinced that the tape-recording was a wild
goose chase.

The paralytic warbled his favourite rendition...
"No need to worry, no need to cry; I'm an undercover
agent working for the F.B.I..."

For the seventh occassion that transition Mathew
ascertained his aspect beneath the half-built window
arch and mounted the carefully laid firestep rostrum.

She had passed him earlier that morning sliding over
debris. The nubile nursing auxiliary had practically
blushed as they almost rubbed shoulders together.

He decided that when the 'jack was sprung' he would
certainly summon up the courage to say 'Good day!'

How many moves after hours when the quarriers had
returned to their nearest and dearest would the sun-
tanned torso of the litter lout have to fool around?
Cough, holler, and call; to loiter in his secret
seedbed to gain her fixed attention.

The spare plot of land was soft-hued as a muzzler.
His precarious platform quivered as he manoevered into
the correct position. The *dolls-house* with its many
exposed chambers lit the occupants of every single room
privately in their dwellings. Wasn't this a *red light
zone* though? Could have been almost anybody.

At last the mystified brunette arrived to mull-over
the box overlooking the juggler, casually champing a
green apple as she did so, and admiring the settlement
from her *rose-window.*

The dirty-Arab signalled from afar. She winced
uncomfortably but decided to outlast his creative urge
invoked for her eyes only. Disproportionately
represented! Little India.

The 'ganger' unzipped his denims and pulled out a
whopper, as the woman leaned forward to take down all
his details.

Thrashing away in the blistering hot sump she glued
her guns to the screen and hovered until he was
beginning to wobble. Cock-Crow!

Spurts of semen sprayed into a dry monsoon as the
punkah-wallah tottered on the pile of sunbaked slabs.

Her upper half seemed to leap clean through the nearby lattice-work shaking her point expressly up and down.

That's no way to treat a lover! There was a pounding in his brain and a scarlet river drizzled onto the waning lunarian's shoulders.

"Hey you! What the hell do you think you're doing down there *Bald Eagle*?" she clattered. He floundered like a Stormy Petrel.

"If you don't stop hawking me you filthy mugwump!" she sternly bellowed at the top of her timbre. "Then I'm going to get you put where you belong!"

It was a wonder that she had not disturbed *Dirty Harry* from his trance. With his Silver Key. Thus departed.

He tottered from his perverted pinnacle quaking like a moose.

A puddle of molten grampus bubbled on the red hot stoney ground.

When he arrived at the summit a *woman dressed in black* was once again consulting the dandiprat.

"Ere, Mathew love," he sniffed. "You're a big strapping lad, built like a *brick shithouse!*"

"What 'ave you been doing?" he drolled, in his drawling Lancashire accent.

XXIII
FALLEN IDOL

The prayer-meeting puffed along with 'Parochial' Pete,
the pimply-faced creep, hamming his lines as confrere
on the side-wagon. A spot-light of stale expressions.

His neutered voice echoed sadly throughout the
establishment among the resplendent *speaking in tongues*
and Yiddish utterances.

Another collaborator arose to announce its meaning,
commended by 'simple' Simon, the ringleader of the
college cult, and prime co-ordinator.

"Let out!" he stipulated. "Let out!" to the moron
still holding out!

"Your human tears must flow in order for our Saviour
to enter your heart and confirm you as a child of the
creator."

The cast of the sect clasped their eyelids and
clenched their teeth.

Mathew slyly undid his latches to focus on the
member with the enormous brown plates also cheating the
syndicate. She yawned so wide he could have built St.
Pauls. Every atom owned by the lord.

The veneer's thick cherry lips motioned a slice of
juice to.roll joyfully over the *diabolical chant* giving
him admirable spectacle to phanta-size.

Once more the evil hand reached out towards the
achromatized church elders swooning in jim-jams.

With a shudder breaking from Felix the nebulous
infection seemed to spread like a virus among the hosts
from the grudging kingdom above.

"Welcome!" he cried..."The lord has been waiting for
you, Mathew, to be solemnly *born again!*"

The sword swallower calmed the weird carnival with a
coded hymn of gobbledegook, and right on cue Upstart
sprang up to the ceiling, floating on his wish, to
interpret the concatenation of circumstances, with

absolute certainty, that his altogether random
occurrance of flukes was without doubt a holy miracle.

The unco-ordinated interpreter deflated to his pew
and requisitioned at the ingress with the silver dish.

"The light of the world sends his *glad tidings*.
Blessed are the meek for they will inherit their
tenement of clay."

Polluting the oppressive atmosphere still further
with his carnal muse the watcher underpinned them with
a concentration of obtuse vibes.

"Some other time," they snarled. "The moment will
soon come when you will be ready to receive the holy
spirit."

'Not on your nelly!' he vowed...

A turncoat Jew daubed in PLO fabrics broke into a brisk
hosanna accompanied on acoustic guitar by the
pedagogue.

"I do hope that you can all come again," he effused.
The listless flock arose from the admirable sense of
well-being to plod sedately through the silent streets
guided only by the star-of-'David.'

There was a month of Sundays to reflect on the
afternoons proceedings...

When he reached the campus at mid-day the head of
department had asked him to explain the cartoon drawn
by *Gollum,* which had been found pinned to his tutor's
bivouac.

A very amusing portrait of the unmistakable power-
lifter climbing a ladder with a hod-full of bricks had
taken some explaining, especially when he had been
three days late in returning for the new term.

Heidi had called in the morning and unwittingly stopped
the whole carry-on..."Do they have harems in the
Universal Church?" he'd asked, but she didn't seem to
follow the essence of his diatribe.

The moon-faced maiden from Finland had spent many
hours trying to persuade him to attend one of their
kirks, but Mathew was only interested in what lay
beyond her skirt...

It appeared as if a nuclear warhead had hit the cockroach cloister when he entered their shared occupation. It was obvious at once that some sort of disturbance had taken place while he was being press-ganged.

Nigel Bates came charging down the stairs in his coffee-coloured underpants with the pebbles of his 'Smartie' gravel *mantra* still sticking to his behind.

"Cholmondesly has just stuck his nut on me!" he roared. "He thinks he knows my number!"

It was unnecessary for Bates to present the large bump which had emerged on his forehead in such a forthright manner.

Thank God he had recovered from the shakes when he had not even been able to hold a glass of pagla pani.

His false bravado resulted from a row about whether *the moon was made of Cheese*.

Following the skirmish in the studio Bates had been swept along the corridoor helped by the size twelve boot of an All Black.

The remains of that huge television set he'd scrawned from the scrapyard had landed at the bottom of the steps like a flying bedstead.

Bates began to spark. He was always very sensitive to changes in room temperature. Said life was a gas.

He darted upstairs for what he could muster to take the sting out of the artful dodger's draining encounter.

Returning rapidly from the mess he pressed his faded copy of *der Spunkenhousen* deftly into his grasp. There was a splodge of green slime on the pigskin, from his last supper we can only assume.

"Good and Evil are simply different sides of the same wad of counterfeit," he advised.

"I think you ought to read the book of changes from a totally unheard of perspective before making up your mind. It's not what goes into the head, it's what you utter out loud which comes from the heart!"

"If you're going to say orthodox things say them in unorthodox clothes."

"You look as if you have been frightened half to death.
What you really need is a damn good quoff. If we hurry
we should be just in time for last orders. There's no
benefit to be had from scoffing rotten fruits. Send
your choppers into uncharted seas and all the rest.
Beware of wicked and corrupt influences."

"Oh, Fuck the 'Holy Ghost,'" he cackled.
"That's excellent!"

"I can't wait until I see Pete tomorrow to give him
'our' Glad Tidings. It's an absolute disgrace what
they have put you through. If I had my way they would
still be feeding them to *the Lions*...the only excuse
god has is that he doesn't exist! It would be far
easier for a camel to pass through the crotch of a
darning tool than for Captain Bob's knob to enter the
gates of Greyfriars."

It was four o'clock in the morning when Mathew suddenly
awoke to find the squatter standing half-naked over
him, munching a pork-pie, and waving an Axe between his
self-defacating fingers...he'd been meaning to put a
lock on that door for ages. Bates swore blind it could
be like a minefield. He wafted his strip of Parchment.

The screaming thing had probably found the weapon
lying around in the *cellar* where he had recently
constructed a dark room.

"What in blazes are you doing Nigel? We were only
pulling your leg."

"I've been having some really spunky dreams!"
blurted Bates in a flurry. He gradually graduated into
delirium.

"Now I'm sure of the worm that never dies; rulers
are meant to be knackered."

"Well, I'll be damned."
There were three numbers smeared in tobacco-leaf across
his thorax. His voice sounded as if it stuttered from
the tip of a distant galaxy, and a shred of corn
projected from his arse-end. If Bates never smoked a
fag in his life, then how come his pincers were forever
covered in nicotine powder? Said he could perform his
own circumcisions. His ear was dripping with blood.

He boasted that he had sprayed graffiti all around the town-hall time-piece.

Spurting in fits and starts the sinister Bates began to describe his bizarre voyage through the mysterious *rose-coloured Ark*, and lifted up his arms to solicit the horrid bite marks.

"I've been taken for a ride by the bloody-bones of the hobgoblins," he barnstormed.

"They returned to whisk me away through the skylight while declaiming loudly in high-pitched harmonies."

"Don't be silly, but of course!" he barracked. "We tossed through the canopy of an enchanted wheel of oak, and landed in the dead-centre of an ancient stone circle..."

"A luminous green eye flickered from the devouring element where we shagged."

"My sire the toadman shelfed us down on tall fungi, where we toasted his health in 'Theakston's Old Peculiar.'"

"It was truly out of this world," he blazed... "They even drink their own piss," he vouched.

"Three cheers for the headless-hunter...down in one! A blasphemous affront to a great many of our polite politicians."

"But he's gone to meet his maker?" Bates scowled and wiped his nose on the back of his hand.

"It was utterly marvellous! There's nothing at all to be worried about on the other side. The hybrids whispered the secrets of immortality in my lug."

"Then we climbed down a small rabbit warren to enter Gae's topaz-coloured Eden."

"I only cancelled my ticket because I accidentally glared at my palms," confessed the deviant pilgrim.

"I have the number now! I have it now!" he whipped. As a result of his amazing encounter Bates was able to move objects at will...

It sounded as if the night owl had been caught wrong-footed when Mathew heard him bleating on the payphone just outside his pigeon-hole.

"Yes mother, it's 'only' me," he heard him whimper. He listened intently and attempted to prevent his mouth from sniggering. "For Christ's sake!" yelled Bates.

A rare-boat of emotion rose and sank as Nigel Bates blasphemed to high heaven.

"Oh, no!" he sobbed. "Not even that. It's terrible, what?"

"How final...do you want me to shoot straight home then?"

He threw the receiver down with such force that it crackled like musketry.

Bates plunged up to his ramshackle dorp with the whey of his vindaloo running down his left shank.

He came flying down the stairs again with the gnomes fishing rod, and his sordes wrapped in a snotty polker-dot, to trammel to the station, along with his mescaline pipe.

"That's it now!" he bitterly rankled. "He's finally got what he always wanted."

"Now he can go to visit the brothel whenever he feels like the fuck-charge."

"My pretty young sister has been slugged by a lion in the path," sniffed the Circumlocutor dismally.

Strange surreal noises plagued his rancorous gullet as Bates set about smudging the puke from his upturned collar.

Down below the oft stray laces of his sneakers had been mischievously tied together. Said he could murder a cereal...

He quickly reverted to rollicking laughter. Mat bade farewell to his adversary at the station and returned to the pile of dirty crockery *nine miles high.*

He persisted in piling a heap of junk between the cooker and the chest of drawers until the queer mountain had reached the desireable height for Farhat the cat and all her grinning peoples.

The blunder of footsteps suddenly bumped down from the thunderbox and the entrance burst asunder.

He winced at the awkwardness of the situation but still received an invite while appearing to change the light-bulb.

"By the way, someone rang for you..." cholered Pete.
    "Coincidentally, I called to see if Nigel would be
attending our next function..."
    "You don't know where he could have been?"
"His curtain was blowing in the draught and his bedding
was completely straight. And some kind of small wooden
'doll' was lying naked on the sheets."

XX1V
FORBIDDEN PLANET

She cleared her swanlike throat and brushed her
bleached blonde shards in the silver glass...smiled her
pretty smile, and at the calling of her mother's voice
charged down the staircase.

She tucked the sky-blue scarf around her neck inside
the orange kagoole, and jumped clean over the steps
onto the *pontoon bridge*.

Everyone's love skipped along the garden boulevards
to visit the *Beast of Hearts*.

Each glowing tulip trebled as she passed and
spreading pollen streamered.

She fixed the sweet red berry above her cerulean
buds and danced along the spangled arches with the cool
breeze bolstering those rosey cheeks...staring into the
light gale with her eyelids on the blink, and causing
tears to roll effusively down her angel face. It was a
rotten trick of hers.

"Summer loving had me some fun..." she warbled as
the 'Go-between' fell into line and finished at the
gate with a bump.

"Get a move on Scallywag!"
The summer snowdrop spun the green mowed lawn about the
congruent flowerbeds, and trotted beneath the splendid
Cherry tree refulgent with its blossom.

She paused to pull up her bobbysocks and received a
lick from the darting *throw-out*.

She giggled and hid inside her coat. Leaning
forward to rap on the knocker she tugged it over her
head.

"I've come to take *Patch* for a walk," she blushed.
"We live just around the corner at number thirteen
also. My name is Lin...what's yours? We were allowed
to play in your garden once before."

"Pardon?" he asked. "What did you say you're name
was?"

"My name is Lin..." she smiled immaculately.
Better ask her again.

"I'm sorry," said the young man. "I appear to be
going deaf in my old age. Did you say they called you
Linn..."

The girl flushed even deeper. "My name is Lin..."
she said and veered towards the drawbridge. Why was he
putting her through the hoop?

"Penny for them," he snapped.
"What?"

"Penny for your thoughts."
"Oh it's nothing," she flushed. "Only I've seen you
once before. You were passing nearby exactly two years
ago. I'd rather have a quid."

"Do you want to come in?" he asked.
"I shouldn't," she replied. "My mum has always warned
me not too since that time with *Mr. Ali.*"

She reminded him of someone but for the life of him
he just couldn't think who. He felt the air of another
planet waft by.

"How old are you?" she teased. "Your hair's
beginning to wave...wave goodbye!" she laughed. "Your
eyes remind me of flowers...cauliflowers! Your teeth
are like stars. They only come out at night."

Suddenly the girl reached into her pocket and pulled
out an enormous ripe tomato.

"Don't tell·my mum will you," she whispered
earnestly. "She doesn't know that I've got one."

She handed him the fruit in her generous outspread
palm.

"A tomato. What on earth?" he complained. She sunk
at his ungrateful response.

"Oh, thankyou," he smiled. "I don't know what to
say."

Mathew galloped to the bay window where the girl
appeared once more.

Her eyes glittered like lapis lazuli as they waved
their magic spell and he pressed his face with
difficulty to the period ventanna until she disappeared
towards *Miles Rough*...

'You are my sunshine, my only sunshine,
You make me happy when skies are grey,
You'll never know dear, how much I love you,
Please don't take my sunshine away.'

Her luscious bare pink thighs spread around his narrow waist as he carried her across furlongs of the verdant fields.

Lindsey's soft repose rested gently on his arch when least expecting a warming ray of sunshine.

A troup of faithful followers tagged along in a band, and as he staggered round the corner her mother lambasted from the other side of the dewdrops.

"For god's sake put her down....she's bigger than you are! What are you? The *pied piper?*"

"I used to go out with a *black-man,*" she bragged. "When we were up in the quiet house we practised Postman's knock."

"Why don't you go steady with Janet?" she asked. "Everyone knows that the farmer's daughter is keen on you. And even Anita likes you. I saw you chatting her up!" she teased. "That day you were on the telly! Hairy chests are sexy..."

They entered her toft and waited until Molly was in the kitchen placing her garments in the tub.

Mr. Barclay retired up to the lavatory to devote some time to his book of oaths. 'Doesn't he have a home to go to?' he enquired.

She flattered him with her ice-blue smile. Taking it in turns they each bent down and kissed the region of their navels, protected by the safe margin of the material. "I dare do it," she laughed. "But only once!"

Swinging her admirable legs up on the sofa she spread them wide and pulled down her navy knickers.

Like a 'sheela-na-gig' she exposed her pouting labia the same way she did on the back seat of the chemistry lab. Could even do the Can-Can.

Mathew stared in disbelief at the size of her giant canyon...she certainly knew how to do a strip-tease.

"Are you disappointed there are no hairs yet?" she asked. Her fingers fluttered over the surface of his zipper..."Now show me your thing!"

"You do it!" She blushed and would not believe he was still unhandselled. "A dirty old man like you," she joked. "You look about seventy five. Keep it inside," she sighed.

"My goodness!" she gasped. "You've got a hairy willy just like William...Quick, pull them up! Is that what it really looks like...long and fat, with the end like a plum?"

"As long as you don't spunk on me!" she said. "It's getting wet inside. Stop before you spunk on me and it runs all down my leg!"

Her gorgeous lamps lit up like burning fires and sparkled with a chilling blue deep in their heart.

Then the informer, Gretel, burst in on them and threatened to impeach her brother, invoking section E. She sneered that sooner or later he'd get copped!

"Look at this girl's face," she glared. "You can't tell me you weren't both up to something!" Lindsey began to cry and cover up her flaming cheeks...

"Do you know that she is a minor?" she fumed. "Leaving her alone with the likes of you. How dare you lead her on," she scorned. "Men like you ought to be castrated, and then it would be too good!"

Gretel hadn't seen anything for certain, but she definitely smelled a rat. Why should he be allowed to get away with it? Nobody else would.

"You can choose your friends but not your family," she disparaged, "just like 'chalk and cheese' they really are. I wouldn't put anything past him."

How many nights thereafter did Mathew supine by their fireside while the male fond girl cavorted in her shorties, flashing her silky stockings, lewdly lifting up her hem and pretending to place a penis into her vagina and St. Elsewhere?

"Will you be coming on Sunday papers in the morning?" She began to weep if he even appeared reluctant.

With the *Evening Star* chanting overhead he turned to glance up at her bedroom window where he knew she would be waving frantically.

As she blew kisses to the true-bad-door beneath the street lamp her mother crooned towards the pretty creature in their modest turret. This was not the silent quintessence of seduction.

She opened her Valentine card while he loitered strictly 'out of limits.'

"Oh, poor Mathew," she said. "Gone and cut his head open. When did he trip over the stone? I must go round to see if he's alright."

Each member of the tribe pulled on a woolly pom-pom hat and arrived glimmering on the mat.

Her young man was still refusing to see visitors no matter how earth-shaking, but for a few seconds they persuaded him to acquiesce.

Mathew painfully exulted as they grinned up from the bier...

Straddled to his back in symbiotic harmony he honked the *Chevalier* tune.

To the mercy of Baal and the holy habit of religion. I swear by almighty god that the evidence I give...

"My mum says it's okay for the time being," she said. "We *can* go together."

"And you will make a good enough chum for our Michael."

"Look at Nicholas!" she roared over the hedge. "That's the pervert who's been *done* for stealing ladies knickers from their washing lines. My mum told me never to talk to him, or go for a ride in his car."

"Girls of that age will go with anyone!"
'You can only dispose of innocence once!'
"Whatever turns you on," she sneered.
She'd keep her mouth shut "for now!"
"You and your bald-headed boyfriend!"
"Why don't you go to hell!" she yelled.
"Do you have to keep saying you're sorry?"

Through every type of season Lindsey and Mathew trammelled cheek by jowl over hill and dale.

'His' grant was spoken for with wine gums. 'She' was born beneath the arrow of a bowman.

"Paul isn't my boyfriend anymore," she declared. "It's you I li...It's you I love best from now on Mathew...promise you'll never desert me?"

"Do you like Fiona? I hate her! She always thinks she's better than us. Did you see how easily he went off with her on the big dipper?"

"You're the only girl for me," he said. "I'm not interested in her or anyone else!"

Lindsey was standing by the willow tree when they knew they were alone...

"Why aren't you married yet?" she asked in fun. She tried to tickle him as they chased around the skirt.

"Marry me then," he joked.
"But you look older than Mr. White."

"Can I meet you again in ten years time?" He simply had to gather the harvest before returning to the *firing-range.*

"In five years my dad says."
Leaving the grain and rain soaked pollen freeborn they retired to the pumping-room tucked away safely in the kush. One drop of semen to a hundred of Blood!

Although Scallywag barked for twenty minutes she was not allowed to watch him train.

Before currenting the wind they wandered expectantly in the shadow of a shade where the sign stood against the far partition; *Pinewood Studios.* It earned him some extra dosh while studying at the *Fart Academy.*

They stood admiring the craftmanship together. Then he suddenly felt her hand sneaking lightly over his bum. A hard task-mistress.

He discovered Infanta to be more than usually coloured.

She began to pipe and purl...

"I must, I must, I must improve my bust!   I will, I
will, I'll make it bigger still! Hurrah! Hurrah!   I
need a bigger bra!" She could even do the splits!
   "*Nitimur in vetitum!*" he ventured.
Knuckling down on the bench she offered to demonstrate
a jape she had recently learnt at middle school.   It
would only take a few seconds while he closed his eyes.
   'Imagine there's a *cluri-chaune* standing in the
centre of my hand,' she propositioned.
   "Now scratch her head! Point to her belly
button...she's wobbling because you tickled her. Touch
where you think the ends of her nipples are...she likes
that! Now put your finger towards her crack."
   At this juncture Lindsey bent over to place her warm
wet mouth around Mathew's outstretched finger...The
surprised digit slipped sloppily out of her
accomodating oriel with a noisy slurp, and he jumped
back at the startled poking feel.
   "I'd give anything to have a suck of your willy
Mathew," she said. Smiling happily she made out a case
with her wayward thumb. "You could get into trouble if
I ever told anyone," she squinted. "But don't worry.
I promise 'not' to kiss and tell."
   Lindsey 'tuatha' lay down the length of the bench
and spontaneously dropped her frilly white knickers
adroitly to her ankles.
   "Lick me out then," she exhorted. "I want to feel
what it's like inside my pussy."
   "Pretend to be asleep," he suggested.
"No! You'll put your hairy willy straight in my
mouth," she insisted. "I've had that sticky lump in me
before...I don't have to!" She pouted disobediently and
exposed her expanse across the *Plimsoll mark*. "Cross
your heart and hope to..."
   Kneeling down between the lush white virgin's legs
Mathew licked around the gleaming hole of the Infanta's
bald crutch.
   It seemed to arouse the pungent odour of her sex.
His old Mahatma tongue pierced enticingly between the
young bay wedge.

Her weeping jib responded with a modicum of gum which
he gently lapped with trepidation. He masticated the
odd pickles of *double Gloucester*, until she panicked
and urged him to halt; "It makes me feel like jelly and
I want to go to the throne-room."

The Infanta's eyes sparkled with excitement and her
autocratic stars seemed to burst into rapture.

She pleaded with him to evince how human semen
manifested itself. He was apprehensive whether he
would be able to satisfy her want and did not wish to
disappoint the iron heel.

Greater Mogul slowly undid his peggies as requested
and she placed her curious hand inside the wrapper.
His penis blushed at the prospect of being guzzled by a
cherub.

"Why do you have to hold it in your hand?" she
complained. "Can't you simply let it go so I can see
your whole length?"

"Show me what spunk looks like," she demanded
intolerantly. "I know that you can! Make it shoot out
of the tag or I'm going home to watch *Blue-Peter*."

Lord of the damned crouching in your secret lair was
this the tender maiden with whom to plight thy troth?

He cajoled her into helping with her firm young
grip...

"You toss it up and down?" she asked. Concentrating
all her attention on the bloated glans so that she did
not miss anything.

"That's to stop your hand from slipping off the
end," he nodded. "Trust me, I'm a medical man."

"No, just hold it still, that should be enough.
There's no need to pull it roughly about like that."
Should he insist she draw tight her flawless white
cornea in case he fluffed it?

Comfortably encircling the erect circumference of
his gentle penis she squeezed and relaxed alternately
as he had instructed.

Her vordant mouth strayed wider than Warrington gap
as she slipped unconsciously forward. A mizzle of dew
leaked from the ferret eye only centimetres from those
lovely baubles.

"Come on! Hurry up!" she scolded tartly from the desk. "I haven't got all day and there's plenty more I could be doing. Tell me when you're going to spunk so I can be ready won't you? Why are you taking so long when I've been holding it for nearly half a minute? It's longer than you said, and now you're just being stupid! I'm doing all the sodding work," she grunted.

The guru exorcised the lucrative limits of his authority and could feel a tingling sensation beginning to roll the clouds. He gave her effort full marks and a bird's eye view.

She slowly pushed out her sipper, procuring a single drop of his emission on the very tip of her tentative probe, and tasted the fluid with a disagree-able mien, as the straining fruit swelled ever further towards its ripening.

With this singularily erotic act *Young Cyrano* in his fleece began to spurt powerfully into the host of heaven. With that he stole her fancy and flung it to the firmament.

Her blazing stars were still mesmerized to the core as she instinctively raced to cover her chomper. With a gipping grunt of her gut her gripper reached especially for her abdomenal area.

He eked-out the chockfull himself before he could comfort her. The cascading continued endlessly before her open gaze. She brayed desperately for her nunky.

Her senses swam and her lush young pins reeled unsteadily. A sickly back-lash distinctly retched and the snow-white face had surrendered its attractive tinge of erubescence.

Between her outspread legs a pool of gippo cloistered on the dry concrete base. Once more she rose to leave as the footsteps of her mother trailed across the yard.

"Oh, mamma, where's my mamma?" she cried through pillars of beatified salt.

"Why didn't you tell me when you were going to drop your load. You promised that you would before we started."

Tears welled-up in those pretty blue buds as he tripped over the dumbell.

"It smells like a pigsty in here!"
They both waved to 'Aunty' Mary drying the dishes through the cabin window and 'sick of the sight.'

Mathew could not suppress the ecstatic smile which spread over his gleaming aspect.

He wanted to hug her joyfully and to celebrate this feeling of great deliverance.

"Is that what really happens inside a woman's body? I didn't know it was going to be like that," she gawped.

"I'm sorry," he said. "I'm really doing my penance...but I never meant to cry wolf. Though that which is done out of true love always has a certain freedom of error beyond the pale of human endeavour."

"Well it's too late now," she gibed. "Oh, don't keep going on about it. You already have, besides, it never really happened!"

She soon tarried with the Piper's tribe as they gathered the black fruit in twilight innocence. The mut with cataracts wandered around the outskirts.

For a moment the indiginous felon strolled with his head above steam. But when it came to push and shove....

A silent dose of rain had bathed the ripened seed with a succulent covering of moisture and within every tiny mirrored globule appeared the distorted shapes of *Tuatha*.

Like a decadent star the fallen hero sank into an ever deeper morass but was still joyously happy.

He desired to pour holy water over her victorious attributes now that *Grendel* had been put to death in daylight hours.

The terra incognita had dared to mutter its moniker; what a triumph to return to Gollum with!

Lead in her pencil. Ink in his pen. White men can't get it up! Boloney.

Said she'd been screwed already by James the Crowbar. You big-bald-beautiful-bastard.

Suddenly she toppled broken-hearted from the step.
No amount of consoling seemed to prevail upon the heart
of the matter. Great balls of tears sprouted from her
pretty germs and plummetted over the water's edge.
    'The darker the berry the sweeter the juice,' it is
said...
    "Tell me what's the matter?" he pleaded. But she
was cast in a terrible scud of water-vapour. Seemed
like worlds apart.
    Only after consultation with Mary would her mother's
visit to the surgeon become common knowledge.
    He placed his arm lovingly around her shoulder when
she said that no-one in her family loved her and
squeezed her gently to his side. Mathew removed a barb
from her hair.
    "But I think the world of you!" he insisted
despairingly.
    "Well, *I hate you!*" she quickly retaliated.

XXV
HEART OF GOLD

When Mary and the 'lodger' evaporated over the cobbles
for another week the *little red riding hood* would sob
from her popcorn-bag in the back seat.

Why on earth was he stranded in *Anticthon*?
Saucy Miss. Gibbon had been telling fortunes in the
gypsy tent at the festival, but no amount of fluttering
her eyelashes could persuade him to renege with her to
the hop.

He won the 'Welly throwing competition' with a throw
of over one hundred and ten feet...but the attractive
form inside the blonde's black bikini filled him with a
sense of trepidation. The Art Miss was learning Hindi.

Mary went bananas when she heard he was planning to
trudge on the stupid paper round after all her scheming
behind the scenes with *thunderthighs*. Lindsey said it
was like trying to get blood out of a stone sometimes.
Could learn anything by heart if he tried.

'There's nothing stopping you,' coaxed the Infanta.
"They've started. They've really started. No they
haven't, I'm only joking," she laughed.

Discharges of *white hot pus*. Gorgonzola? "Cross my
heart and hope to die," she said.

"Not with that little strumpet!" Back another inch,
"Noddy, look it's Noddy!" screeched the local kids.
"It's Noddy in his woolly hat. What's he hiding
underneath?"

Friends and neighbours boggled at their windows.
Butterscotch memories melted through the cornflake
blaze of festoons.

And what are little girls made of? Sugar and spice,
and all things nice...the sun danced in her eyes.

"I like men's willies," she giggled. "But I don't
like their hairy balls. I know it's wrong, but it's
right." And when they were up, they were up, and when
they were down, they were down, and when they were only
half-way up they were neither up, nor down...

111

A scarlet flicker of heat filtered through the charcoal sunrise and he made her his own with the *band of gold*.

There was a twinkle in her eyes and her hair dazzled him with its radiance as if love had repulsed the sands of time. A long long time ago. The Happy Prince.

'Though this jewel fades, my love for you will never burn in flames.'

"I'm dreaming of a white Christmas."
"Make a wish," he said, as if they were snapping bones. A ray of light caught the solitary heart as she danced around the totem with her eyes fixed on the rebound.

"Yippee, it fits," she cried, leaping into the air. She splashed her sunshine like a merry bowl of rhymes.

The tiny fairy queen waved the plain motif magnanimously at the spur and his breast soared like a bird. There was a flighty look in her eye as he attempted to share a knotty point. She tossed away her daisy-chain. Whose heart was made of pure pure gold.

"Even if I fall out with you I still get to keep it," she assumed. There were stars in her eyes.

"Kiss me a third time, and I might turn into a woman," she conceded. Marooned in the marshes of the Moon...

"Thirteen is going to be lucky for someone! If I granted you three wishes what would they be?"

"I don't want to see you for a few days," he said. "Have I done something wrong?"

But there was no mountain he would not climb, no valley where he would not chase the magical blue falcon, because, when Lindsey smiled at her Mathew, he felt as if he had just been kissed by a beam of golden sunshine. Was it not for you, the glacier, today, exchanged its grey for roses?

Through harvest years they turned and changed, navigating the vortexed land together, with an odd hanger-on who disappeared after a period on the Odyssey...her mother becoming unduly suspicious over piggy-back riders in the white stuff.

Molly arrived to ask Mathew on holiday with the family.

But she still appeared anxious when her daughter
flashed her new signet ring.

"It's harmless enough I suppose. I knew someone
like you at her age and he turned out okay....I think
Mathew is a very fine young man," she gleamed, and
smacked his bottom mischievously.

Molly placed her arm around his shoulder line.
"You don't know what you're missing! He's brave, hard
working and trustworthy. Not like some of the
layabouts you see in town. He's got a good future
ahead of him I'm sure."

"But take care with her," she warned. "Lindsey is
very immature for her age...you'd be surprised, even
though she is so self-assured and thrustful. As long
as you never touch her," she said. "Because you know
what will happen if you ever do!"

"Don't look so serious," she kidded. "I'm not as
green as I am cabbage looking! Don't squeeze the fruit
unless you're purchasing. The birds and the bees."

Mary scrutinized the rare metal article with
impatience.

"You are an idiot!" she scorned. "Buying a girl of
that age such an expensive overlay."

"You know what 'he' thinks about that sort of thing.
There better not have been any visitors while I have
been away."

"But what about 'his' behaviour with Felicity?"
Mary renewed her wide expanse and hissed just an inch
away from his pod. Just in case the broadcast was
being scrambled in his mixed-up befuddled brain.

"Don't give me any of your cheap tricks!" she
scoffed.

"Can't you see she's nothing but a wily *gold-digger.
Have you lost your sodding marbles?* She's man mad,"
she said.

Then she threatened him with the moral ogre of
common-sense and human decency.

"Go and live with the Barclays if they'll have you,"
she repeated.

"Let them find out what you are really like inside."
"But get out of my hair once and for all and leave us

in frigging peace. And don't you start talking like
'that,'" she warned. "Gretel's new boyfriend has a
theory about men like you. Just you try talking to him
like you do to me."

At this moment the pygmy in rat's wings began
sparring like a flyweight.

"Love her," she barracked. "How can anyone in their
right mind say that about a twelve year old child?"

She shattered the back of his skull with a flat
crack from her palm. Said she'd reached the bitter
end. Held a diploma in how to re-write history.

With the charms of an all conquering *Amazon* Mary
swept into command. Takes not a blind bit of notice!

"Monstrosity, when are you going back to college
instead of tramping the streets with her?" she
bellowed. "You don't want to be around when she starts
experimenting with men!" Of course.

"No son of mine is going to be known as a reprobate.
Who ever heard of a grown man paying so much attention
to an insignificant whelp. The lawn wants mowing, the
roses clipping, and the soil needs tilling," she
fermented. "You're only half as good as Esmerelda's
son. Muscle always turns to fat."

"Then you won't be surprised if I only act half as
good! Have you got a cough?" he asked.

"Don't you even care about her reputation as soon as
this is over?" bolted Gretel. "Don't you realize you
are fighting a losing battle? In years to come she'll
look on you with loathing. Box his ears for him
someone." Whatever happened to her little boy?

"Just look at his eyes!" implored Fiona. "Do you
love her? No, of course that's *impossible.* Are you
fond of her then? Is she your friend? Well, that's
alright then. That's quite 'normal.' As long as there
isn't anything else going on which you haven't told us
about."

The *Milesian* woman made a lunge at him with the
rolling pin and connected on his *calcium bonnet.*

The milkjug standing conveniently on the tray nearby
was emptied over his bald spot.

"Get the message!" she cried. "Go to the other side
of the room!"

Lindsey appeared rather taciturn about the invitation but he tried to accept her word that she was only going at his sister's request. The vernacular granted as part of the *round to buy her friendship* had been used to purchase an expensive gold fountain pen. She said that it was none of his business who it was for and that his constant questioning was infuriating.

When he left her at the gate as if butter wouldn't melt she turned and hurried up the drive without a single wave, looking more captivating than ever in her high heels and mauve paint.

As promised he returned at ten o'clock with Jonathan, who stood with Mathew at the bottom of the stairs waiting for the missing guest to materialize.

'He' was the only lad in the house it transpired. Once more his sister *Cheryl* charged up the steps and clattered on his bedroom door next to the bathroom.

"Quick, hurry up in there you two. Your dad's here, and he's looking rather sore."

After a pause of several minutes the key eventually turned in the lock and the couple emerged reluctantly to face the music. As she led the procession her Prussian eyes glittered like watered gems. She was flushed like the days on which she was truly tickled pink. A chorus of 'Ooh, what have you two been doing?' met them as they slowly descended from above. "As if we don't know!"

"We didn't do anything, honest," he occulated. "So it's you who coughs up the loot."

"I don't think that Mathew is my friend anymore," she intonated...

The Rainmaker brought the house down.

The blizzard was veering westward as he assured the young woman that all was *hunky-dory.*

He would only be a few minutes more before returning into the house to help her crack a bottle.

He hurried through the freezing downpour.

Through the furnace of the *French Windows* he could
harbour his strange obsession while the honoured guest
tinkered with her irons on the grate.

From the pumping-house purdah he shuffled furtively
in his Mackintosh.

Deep in the *Marish* cold Mathew pedantically peered
round the edge of the frame.

A narrow chink of light crossed his gules from the
warm interior of the lounge.

She floated round the uncertain circle of the kiln
like a vixen chastised with sting-rays.

He jumped back suddenly as she passed, not wishing
to be exposed at such short notice.

Her cloak-and-dagger eyes searched the miserable
void for sparks and settled on the walls covered with
seasonal greetings. Her recent betrothal had allowed
her partner a permanent refuge.

One by one she worked her way around the jewelled
interior, turning the covers.

From time to time she paused to ponder through the
barrier of the velvet water line.

As she neared the '*Place of Sob*' his lungs burst
like a pair of clapped-out bellows, and she knelt down
on the oriental rug with the occasional glance towards
the rustic. Veird scenes inside the gold mine!

Who was the crooked demon glaring in the glass?
Which devouring spirit shuddered in the pouring hail.
She stared in disbelief at the mantel.

Uncannily obscured by the dim light from the orb the
fly-blown canker-worm, puissant with pent-up need,
pressed his sordid glans against the dreary lens which
masked his faint reflection.

If cruel fate should not permit our angelet to
return...the sky seeks you out, and the wind and clouds
press higher in the blue, longingly they crowd aloft in
search of you.

Her mouth hung open and gasped for oxygen. Was it a
slummy or just some foul thing in high dudgeon?

Caught in a shadowland outside the winter's door the
daring fiend lurched precisely into the aperture of his
dangerous liaison. She seemed as if her mind was cut

by winsome cares, and became overtly interested in the *magic of the cards.*

At last a great slurry and an even greater outpouring of slime issued from the tunnel of his penis end and splattered against the pane. He quickly melted into the dilating fog from where he had lugubriously emerged. Was it the chilling return of a 'has-been?' Nor heaven peep through the blanket of the dark?

His buck-basket had been rifled and the perishable goods vanished like spit in the rain.

XXVI
THUNDERBOLT

Awakening from recurring nightmares of filthy vermin
thriving beneath rotting floorboards in the basement,
he called out for his mother in the sweat stained
environment...

Clarissa had calmly continued typing her 'curriculum
vitae.' It had been seven long months of pins and
needles since the 'dies nefastus' of the rogue Carol
Singers, the day before Yule-tide.

The attractive archivist had turned to scrutinize
his eccentric behaviour at the edge of the living room
floor where he dropped a clanger. Had the growler been
worrying sheep again?

"Ooops!" she cried, and reached for her tippex.
He rejected her cordial invitation even when she
complained she was lacking a suitable escort.

'*Sater venter non studet libenter*,' he remarked.
Knock! knock! "Who's there? Lindsey who...?"
"Can I come in?"

They peeped through the letterbox, they peeped in
the hall, and any other place which had peep-holes...

From tiny seedlings mighty Oaks do crash through car
window-screens! Love her to death. Shoot the apple
from her head.

At the fuel-pump station an Irish *tinker* had asked
the manager if the *Buckfast* 'Flasher' ever exposed
himself while on active duty.

Then the rough and ready hoydens had actually
appeared at the house and been invited inside.

It was a malign attempt to gain a bird's eye view of
the pervert who had defiled their lovely Catholic
daughters.

Mary immediately began proselytizing as if her mouth
was on fire. Step into line there!

Mr. Mullins had pointed to the *wicker chair* standing
behind the kitchen door.

He declared its awful presence triumphantly.

His terse young son casually nodded as if the case was proved beyond all reasonable doubt.

"Was he pissed out of his mind?" quoffed the Tinkerman bloated with moral indignation.

Otherwise it would be unthinkable to withdraw the charge since the matter was so indisputably serious.

"Oh! my god, he'll never get another job now!" she fretted. "We do our level best you know, but there's something the matter with him."

"He was going to go into teaching," she blubbed. "He's much too shy to do such an objectionable thing. Not another sound out of you! It certainly isn't natural. One would like to say."

"I'll never be able to hold up my head at the 'Women's Institute' again. What a *terrible scandal!* Gretel will go mad."

It was an absolute charm to see her expression as the *party snoopers* departed in a much happier frame of mind. They'd even refused his gift of the stereo.

When he had returned that evening from a rare reconnaissance mission with Jonathan they had questioned him on the earlier encounter. Was he a copper in plain clothes asked the customer?

"An Inspector called but wouldn't tell us what it was all about," glared the lodger. "Only that a very grave incident had arisen which involved a *missing person.* He'll be calling again later to see about your alibi."

"Perhaps it was a burglar?" they said. "Are all our doors safely bolted and secured?"

Even the lodger had been under suspicion, until they had matched him with the perfect description; *Bald, bandage, approximately fifety.*

The part-time *balloon dancer* and *bouncer* arrived *with the woman dressed in black* grinning like a Cheshire cat. In view of the gravity of this offence.

Felt as if he had received a hefty blow in the midrift. Two wrongs do not make a right. He was asking for it! ; that ...

The constable stepped lucratively into the kitchen armed with the concepts of even-handed what ought to be.

Inspector Drip-white ticked-off all his details while he listened to the accused indicting himself with every crazy sentence.

He stated that he was certain of the culprit. The woman from Sunhill stared blankly forward as her chief collaborator read him his rights.

"Anything you say will be taken down and used in evidence." Why on earth was he wearing the three-cornered stetson?

The lodger suddenly went haywire and stormed up the stairs to pack his bags at once. She accused him of totally ruining their remunerative affiliation.

"The dirty bastard. Anything but that!" he shrieked. "We'll have to leave the area."

Mathew's attempts to explain were met by stoney silence. What a way to celebrate one's 'coming of age.' Though I waltz through the valley of death.

"Tell them you had nothing to do with it," insisted Mary. "Stand up for yourself and convince them you are *innocent.*"

"Ask them what part of your anatomy you are meant to have *exposed*. Launch a petition to find out why they only called at our house."

"Your *penis!*" he coyly noted. "You exposed your *penis* before the choir showed a clean pair of heels."

To everyones surprise Mathew quoted the occassion of their fellow officer in the 'Dog and Gun.'

"Please make sure you notify us if you intend to leave the country. A hairdressing appointment? How much?" No right to rob the unadulterated?

"The *shite of the earth*," he muttered, as they manoevered towards the exit.

The constable insisted that the final outcome was dependent upon whether his *Pace-maker* had enough data to bring about a *successful prosecution.*

Despite the growing *ship of spies* he faithfully

complied to increase his decreasing chances.

"Am I a Prostitute?" she'd asked.
"Don't be silly," said Mathew. What on earth was the world coming to?

"Are you dying?" she smirked. "Is that all it is then?"

When he told her the filler she nearly hit the roof.
"You stupid idiot!" she said. 'How could you have acted without due care and attention. I don't believe it either,' she said..."You were on your way down from the bathroom? Were you born in a field?"

He had anticipated his name appearing in glorious print, and a colour coded snap.

"A 'Flasher!'" Mollydod cooed. "I didn't think that you were that capable."

"Make the most of your semester"...then a fuitine was totally out of the question?

As he stood nude in the shower she turned on the hot water tap over the Father-of-Steps.

"Get one together! Look at that!" she quivered.
"It's standing to attention. Let me see you piss or are you going to *fuck me*?"

Infanta led him into the cabin where she first let down her intimate particulars.

She was careful that he didn't touch her with his *light companion* or kiss her when he was filled with fondness.

"You ought to see our Jonathans'!" she gasped. "I wish he'd let me sleep for once."

She attempted to force his sensitive glans between her flaps.

"Avast!" he yelled. His 'Plummy! had been skinned alive.

Then she complained again. Nothing was mentioned about going on the pill. Or the scud marks on her frillies.

"Shove harder and get into rhythm, I'm doing all the work"....had she already been through the motions?

The door suddenly moved but she slammed it quickly shut again.

"You're gonna get done!" shouted William.

He'd said that Mathew was too good for her from the very beginning. "I'm telling my ma...na, na, na na na!"

"Mathew's only showing me his etchings." She pressed some caramel under the drop and stared with awe at the colour of his scotch. Peek-a-boo!

One wet finger did it very well...two were even better; she reached down to grip his wrist and guide the hand in closer.

The *bald* crutch-head lock-jawed as her eyes sunk into a 'Wonderful land.'

Poking progressively towards the stars she moaned and deepened, fixing his hand even more firmly than before as he concentrated wisely on the task.

Her gorgeous buds began to flutter between hawk and buzzard. Afraid of being struck-off?

She seemed oblivious to the customer and groaned like a bomber as she rapidly reached climax...tiny spots of grume stained her knicker-lining.

"If that's what an orgasm is like, I want to do it some more!" she murmured. "I can't wait until I get to bed tonight when I can pull down my blanket!"

Lindsey pushed the *trinket* into his raincoat pocket for a mangled summer evening.

"Are you taking us all down to the woods to eat our pic-nic at dinnertime?" she asked.

"And remember, no mis-behaving yourself! I hope Reverend Brown doesn't see us together in the bushes. I'm tired of saying that you're just my brother's friend.

"If you go down to the woods today, you're sure of a big surprise," she trilled.

"If my man knew about this she might think you were really naughty!" she teased.

   *   *   *

"Done this sort of vile thing before?" asked the Peeler as they checked the station records..."He's *clean!*" the factotum comfirmed (computers never lie!).

"There's no-one on our patch who looks remotely like the suspect."

"Did you hope to turn her on? Her husband's in the force and he's twice the size of you! It was all I could do to persuade him not to give you a bloody good drubbing!"

Like putty in their hands the student agreed to every single term. Frontal lobotomy. Chip on his shoulder a mile wide.

Guilt ridden. Bogged down with guilt. Blood on his fingers. Consumed with guilt. Guilty as fuck. Guilty as charged.

"I hate these left wing commi bastards," stormed the sergeant..."You're not one of those are you?"

"Of course not!" he snapped.
The virgin's prickly heat spread over his entire coin-face and down his back.

It felt as if his whole body was becoming a *red hot giant*, and he didn't know where to look in the frame to do himself justice.

"I believe that this is truly a *flash in the pan*. You won't do it again after this shock to the system. Best make a sincere apology and get yourself sorted out."

"Do you have a steady girlfriend? How long is it since you had a really good bang?"

Did he confess?...'I'm a virgin, and I have been all my life'..."It's been three whole weeks since I last had *an intimate coupling*," he paltered.

"Three weeks you say?"
"She swears that you had an *erection*. Would you deny or dispute this fact? Were you masturbating, come on admit it, we haven't got all day to mess about! I have several other *good eye witnesses* who are willing to come forward."

The hare-lipped *head of vice* supined coolly on his swivel and scrutinized his transfixed guest.

"Okay, we've finished for the time being," he gesticulated (had he passed the interview?). "Belinda will chaperone you back to the scene of your crime to pick-up your Post Office van."

"Just sign a full confession and we will send the
results as soon as possible"

Mathew quickly donned his signature in order to
return from this rough coinage. Who needs a solicitor
when you're *right up Queer Street!*" 'Bent as a nine
bob note,' as Bobby used to say.

She led him into the staff car park where he
automatically climbed in the front of the *Panda* beside
his host. He continued in conversation until they
approached the Chemical plant.

"You should know better," she nodded
sympathetically...then he noticed that she too had
broken into a hot flush.

He turned and watched her beaming face as they
travelled along the now deserted streets still bathed
in evening sunshine.

"Just don't do it again!" she warned. "Find
yourself a nice girlfriend. It shouldn't be too
difficult. But I can't promise she'll withdraw her
allegation. Apparently you were making a nuisance of
yourself since the start, although I'll convey your
deepest remorse. No, I don't think it will be a good
idea if you told her so yourself."

The short skirt had lifted well up the lithesome
blonde's admirable young thighs, which beckoned his
lazy hand with a covering of creamy silk...

Should he break the habit of a lifetime and make a
pass? Whether to leave it another minute or move his
hand idly across while he still festered unfulfilled.

Good sense seemed to have prevailed for the moment
but the *young woman dressed in black* seemed to sense
the strong vibes he was despatching by male.

When they arrived at the row of cottages beside the
loading bay the yard was empty of the jeering crowds.

How cliche-ridden it had been continually patrolling
the building's circumference, until the hobnobbers had
strolled onto the terrace, on this, his last day 'on
the job.'

As he closed the door behind him he peered toward
Belinda's Noon and smiled.

Mathew apologized once more for making such a spectacle of himself. She simply shrugged her shoulders and pushed her foot firmly on the pedal.

Mathew stepped away from the kerb, careful that he did not disturb the flat cap now resting on his bonce. He swayed along the rusty pavement like unoiled clockwork as people hurried from their doors and slammed them shut.

He had a final gander towards the Riding Stables where the spectator's lusty eyes had studied him for hours. Her sister had only been a-watching for half that time.

Like Beckett's 'Catastrophe' in his 'Flasher's Mac' he loitered with new nostalgia in the region of his favourite perch.

It seemed only minutes before he had spent all his lunch time trying to attract the secretary clearing the files, sitting on the thunderbox sucking his thumb with the door open-mouthed.

Like a hammer from the sky the horserider had jockeyed like a thunderball.

He had tottered from the pile of pallets stacked man-high and sprained his ankle.

The tygress in her mid thirties had obviously never seen a semi-erect penis in her life before so she ran screaming through the rows of workmen like a siren.

"Take a good look at his repulsive clock!" she bawled pacing up and down the den with her forked tongue lashing vehemently.

"How can we sleep safe in our beds with a *dangerous monster* on the loose!"

When he walked calmly into the house suffering from catatonic shock only Gretel noticed the bright cherry on his cheek...but then he was always sun-bathing. Serves him right the so-and-so.

The *herald on set* was reporting a television *newsflash*...and sexy Miss. *you-know-who* had escaped on a majority verdict for wielding a whetted blade on the march.

Blackbeard had been safely captured after wearing false number plates...they interviewed Ryan Starbuck as a close neighbour, and asked him his impression of the mad pandemic necromancer. Frigid, or Sandra, or both?

'Just an ordinary sort of chap, never really spoke much out of turn,'...on his way to the ritual abattoir.

"You're home rather late tonight?"
Gretel instructed him to read one of the passages in her manual.

"Neurotics always hurt the people who are most trying to help them! Although you certainly haven't much to offer even that vindictive little hussy."

"But it's only the 'myth of mental illness'," he stressed. "I've always compared myself to the matchless of this world!"

Mathew wasn't in the mood for her hortative. He bolted up to his dorp and began playing with his pipe.

In the garden below Juliette was folding up her deck chair. Bad weather on the way?

She was a delicate blushful of curls with the complexion of peaches and cream.

Through the green leaves and the apple blossom he admired her natural tendencies as he did so often when they were in tryst.

He approached from the edge of his seat to the windowledge, revealing his titanic erection and smacking away as expeditiously as possible. Consistent with his strawberry mark.

Juliette turned as she pulled the wooden clothes pegs from the line and glanced in his direction right on cue... Bashing the bishop!

How many secret gardens had he sojourned below the arc of the covenant, or in the privacy of their *boudoirs*, where a note-book on his bedside cabinet contained the results of his challenge?

His huge shiner spurted the mounting proceeds of his edification through the yawning hiatus.

A downpour of hotstuff glaired over the cradle of branches and ended their life on the low tide. Q. C. - Quality counts!

Mary insisted he borrow the lodger's finest three piece; it was badly fitting, but it was important to create a good impression. Was he attending an exchange of nuptial vows? Pawn to king four.

Before you could say 'John Robinson,' 'Bald Eagle' was sitting bolt upright in the dock beside the burly *Big Blue Whale*...Fatso had met him with a grin in the foyer. In court number 6 the pale pukey face of the *white dwarf* gaped from the backseat while the merry Tinkers pawned around their confident barrister.

A mixed party of teenage truants crammed into the public gallery to view the debacle, and listened intently to the 'victims' giving evidence. Strength in numbers. They tittered melodically when the officer read out the wicked deed.

When the clothes were off his dickie-bird didn't even come out of the cuckoo clock to sing.

It was the incorrect address, but the defendant's representative from '*Goose, Gander & Gosling*' said it didn't matter one jot. He was only 'splitting hairs.'

Hated and reviled by all who cocked their eyes the dirty flasher trembled as the sport of wind and waves...like a 'bookful of gossips.'

Gretchen described how he had offered them fifety-p to sing 'Away in a Manger,' and how he wedged the chair against the door while he went into the living room to flaunt his ugly penis. Not allowed to wolf-whistle!

At this point there was a thunderous fanfaronade of plaudits and a storm of jubilant flag waving, but it was only a militant tendency I expect.

"Did he do anything while he held it in his hand?" she billetted her second witness. Her voice was filled with melancholy for their potash. In check.

Mathew couldn't help waving across to their kraal, which was duly noted by the Justice of the Peace. He flashed them his Eddie Murphy smirk.

"I didn't see, it was too dark," she said. "I only looked because my sister said that I should do."

"Did the accused have an erection?" she asked. Then they had to go and explain what all that meant.

The precise details of his adamant penis were discussed before the teeming oceans.

"Why should you concoct a story like this?" she tendered. The congregation turned to scrutinize his *alien presence*.

Then it was Mathew's turn to take the stand. He read out the chips in his best public speaking voice and swore feign allegiance to the captive.

Before the hearing he described how he came to be serving up his broth that evening. Under cross examination there was a burning in his breast when the lady asked him if he was using his organ to obtain unacceptable gratification: but did not...

He stammered when he came to the prose where the girls had kicked open the turnstile. And he paled when Mary Moonighan blew in her hanky.

The highly experienced aid rushed to his side. "We must have the name involved" he vexed. "Why do you think those girls were conducting a vendetta against you." Can't castle!

"And just who is this...this Lindsey?" asked the leading Magistrate huffly. "What has she to do with all this coming and going, mainly going?"

"How old is she...thirteen? Is she your girlfriend? Do you seriously expect the court to believe that you are having a relationship with a thirteen year old minor?" Queen takes pawn!

Mathew was on tender hooks as the three pillars of the establishment retired to deliberate.

Postman Pat had already passed on his recorded telegram that same morning for a return appointment in three weeks time. Another feather in his cap!

Rumours circulated in the public gallery that there would be further complications.

A spectator called out "Baldy!"
"It's fifety-fifety," sibilated the postulant. "Let's pray that they will be lenient."

The hydra returned with the verdict; *guilty*...a hundred pound fine! The depraved person must have been the only onlooker who wasn't smiling. His ego grinded to a halt.

Once more Mary was vindicated in her views about his
true character though she offered to stay on his side.

As he walked from the court building in the centre
of town a flurry of mocking taunts echoed behind him.

The tinker woman leapt on his back with her running
commentary. Check-mate.

"Do you see my poor girls!" she screamed, pulling
their hair. 'Look how chaste and vulnerable they are!'

"You're a very wicked and evil man. All I want is
that you apologize for your disgusting behaviour and
swear it will never happen again," insisted Mary.

She stated that if he continued pumping iron he
would surely shrink in height.

Mathew turned to stare at the two gleaming wretches
in their neatly pressed jungle-green. Expect she
already had a bun in the oven. But when push came to
shove. Cortes burnt all his ships...

He recognized them both instantly as 'Southern'
Milesian Women, with the medal of carnal knowledge
already etched in the corners of their crooked leering
mouths. Three rings for the elven kings...

Two enormous *brillo pads* were no doubt growing like
hell over the *black holes* between their opprobious
hips! Mudslinger!

Lindsey hardly batted an eyelid when he said that he
had been found responsible. She simply asked for a
rise in her pocket money. Filthy animal!

"I'll let you fuck me if you wear a *black johnny*,"
she whispered. "Okay, Dr. Fox, show me what ya got!"

All afternoon the man in the woolly festoon
whimpered paranoically whenever the pair locked eyes on
a handsome young stud. Wet her knickers as soon as
look at him. Now Prancer, now Dancer, now Vixen...

After all the fun of the fair she demanded another
ice-cream. Knight takes rook!

Mathew handed her the cone careful not to drop
it....Lindsey tipped it carelessly in the gutter and
carried on up the lane.

His hopes were hanging on a heartbeat as he rapidly
approached crisis point.

But it was no use shutting the stable door after the horse had bolted.

When they arrived home in the kitchen the 'lodger' was urinating in the basin.

Lindsey edged closer to the bottom of the stairs with a lustful ardour on her fresh young face.

"Cor!" she said. "Get a load of him. He's a nice bit of stuff and right. Try running your fingers through 'his' hair."

The 'lodger' returned doing up his trousers as she feasted her eyes on his cock bulge...he sneaked out towards his clandestine appointment with Mary safely absent.

His Sicillian charm bore down on them like a cart of shite and onion. But his 'but' was higher from the ground than normal men.

"Now that's what I call fit!" she motioned, and pretended to pat where her eyes concentrated most. Tit for tat killings. Hah!

Then the music was finally over...he prepared to raise a storm and fight them tooth and nail.

Mathew flew into a rage and accused her of taking him for a ride...Superfluous to requirements. She had set her sights on greener pastures.

The words so sincerely sneered had a ring of truth in them. Like peas in a pod.

"'Your' girlfriend!" she mocked. "Don't be such a broody hen. Alright," she sneered. "Always said you were a meanie." Pull the other one, it's got bells on.

"Keep your hair on! Wouldn't fancy you if you were the last man on earth. Shouldn't mock the afflicted."

The rainmaker glanced at her friend as if he'd fallen off a flitting as he fluttered like a duck in thunder and his complex sonnets didn't rhyme. Said she was 'shagged out.' Always showing her up.

"Your not going to cry again?" she sniggered. "Why can't you leave me bloody well alone. I'm never touching you again. Didn't think I was going steady!"

"And he's bigger than you are puffta."
"Why don't you get a girlfriend your own age," she assailed..."if you can that is!"

Said she'd blown him totally out.

Though he promised them a milky way Phoebe slammed
the shaft behind her and she promptly *fell from grace*,
like a barrel of tear gas to the bottom of the ocean.

When the music's over baby, turn out the light, turn
out the light. The spirit left him...

Molly's bloated face crushed exigently against the
porthole attempting to catch a look in the place.

The bouquet of forget-me-nots had been tossed in the
trash-can, and on the blower the misfit had been too
distraught to speak. You've got to run before you can
walk. His batonic hands quavered like a burst
conductor's Brahm.

Always with a ciggy in her cake-hole. Wasn't the
sort of woman who took 'no' for an answer. Watch your
language! This is the last straw.

The tapster put her arms around him, and said that
though they were still friends, it was better for all
concerned that he no longer attended the reception.

She was wearing the 'Heart of Gold' on her finger
because her daughter said the metal was too irritating.

"It's just for now," she added softly, "I'm sorry,
but in time you'll both get over it!"

"You can't expect to hold a girl to promises she
made so young."

"The path of true love never runs smoothly. That's
a fact of life! Give it a while and then just say
hello when ever you meet. Completely ignore her for a
change. Anyway, you'd need a buffet to kiss her."

"I can't force her to take you on board. For now
it's over and done with. It gave her the hump when you
called her a *tart*. She needs her own freedom to skim
off the cream."

"If you found a more suitable companion you'd need
no reminding. We can't always get the one we
desire...but don't start making up stories."

She was certainly startled when he told her that he
had indeed been struck by a charge of electricity...but
all her family were a cut above the rest.

Someone had even whipped the time-piece.

"Personally I don't care what they do in private, as long as they don't scare the horses."

She showed him the door. Tiny bit camera shy. Set off like a six year old looking for his sock.

He pulled the camera strap over the shoulder of his leather bomber jacket and wanted to hug her so much that he thought of nothing else...knocked the stuffing right out of him.

When he sat down in the queue the licence dodger eventually gave breath. It was like watching the formation of a snow crystal through a microscope. His pulse seemed to quicken.

"Press Photographer?" he asked, nodding at the Pentax.

"Only for the 'News of the World!'" soft-pedalled Mathew.

Just before dinner time the snapshotting dude was summoned into number 6 court as the final entrant in their group.

With his dome flapping like a ragged patchwork quilt the ugly monstrosity loped like a squiffy mechanism. His heart in a silvery cage. Rood-loft.

He entered the wooden pulpit beside the pews to strut and fret his hour upon the planks. Blushing to be encountered with a cloud. She howled like a bitch bringing herself off.

Once again he was staggered by the extravagant luxury of the proscenium arch which paled all other dressings into insignificance.

This grossly obnoxious farce unwound with unmitigated opulence. Step into line! She showed him the door! Choose who she bloody well wants.

The usher who had been making such pleasant conversation quickly averted her eyes.

"That you did openly, lewdly, and indecently, with intent to harrow the anvil, expose your erect *penis* outside her Riding Stables....." contrary to the *vagrancy* act of 18...something or other.

Thank the lucky stars. Once again the chamber was free of blasted reporters. Retracting his Sigma.

And they said that 'lightning couldn't strike twice' as
he teetered in the dock place. Burst through the
stratosphere. Drop the dead donkey.

"And this is his first offence!" stated the
prosecuting attorney. Stand to attention! Looking for
a showdown? Never drunk on duty.

But as fortune would have it the same burly *Big Blue
Whale* occupied the stand next to him and walked calmly
forward after a few seconds hesitation. Why do all the
Plods have size twelves?

He whispered something odd inside the old man's ear.
Only doing the decent thing. Another bloody prodigy.

"It doesn't count!" he heard him say, shaking his
head, as they settled the matter under duress.

Like a *Gordian knot* scud under bare poles Mathew
tottered in the kiosk with no lack of courage.

Calling occupants of inter-planetary craft. Fish-
faced enemy of the people! Dirty-Den the role model.

The prosecutor indicated that the defendant would
like to offer a few token words in his own defence to
explain his gross abandonment of privilege.

The law required that he be punished by small fire
through a deckful of tropical runes.

Greatest dispensation since the days of Manu.
Perhaps a stiffer sentence would teach him the error of
his ways? Just ignore him and he might go away.

One of the great unwashed. At any moment he
expected to be swept under the carpet.

Out streamed a pack of lies. The *magistrate* leaned
over with a superlative gleam and coyly flashed her
pendulous bosom.

Without reference to a pin or a speared clay effigy.
He squeezed the soft brown owl and held the diplomatic
baggage in his other pad entitled 'Catching
snowflakes.'

A sexual albatross around his neck...stick a pipe in
its gob, nail its foot to the flipping deck. What a
carry on! A fly on the wall. She was dying for it!
"The dirty old git!"

Victim's 'support.'
My dearest Linnet, it ran;

- - -

Here is the letter I've been meaning to send you,
meaning to send you for such a long time now.
I know when you read it, I may be dead...
I may be dead for such a long time now.
But read it, I know that you will one day!

Do you remember when I carried you quite far?
I was loaded with scales but did not think twice,
Oh, what a pretty girl always to me!
I felt very tender, I only felt tender,
and penned the way some porters do...

If ever I hurt you, which I know was not seldom,
then you'd climb and come round with the tide.
From *Whitecastles* I swung you, and sweetly embraced
you, forever I hoped this would be!
But then I grew serious, and you frowned with sad
Autumns, though I should, I never quite understood
why...

But there's something quite often, I meant to beseech
you, which tossed like a leaf in my mind.
Will you quite often, or just for a moment...
will you please *be my bride*,
will you please *be my bride*?

Though I once left you, to shelter your secrets,
and for once march on alone with your cares,
You never quite left me, you never deserted me,
if I could, I'd just like to explain;
I loved you, I love you, I always adored you,
and think of you where ever I glide.

Justice has been done.

"Only jealous!" hissed the Infanta.

XXVII
WICKER MAN

"White man speak with forked tongue!" squirmed the unsentimental Nigel Bates, who appeared about to eviscerate another of his smouldering *Cobra* skins.

"I suppose you've been indulging in some more of your cardio-vascular exercises by the look of you."

A *Blackhole* had materialized in the septic armpit of his decrepit Afghan coat, and he boasted about not having his hair cut professionally since he was a *page boy*. Now he called himself the 'last of the Mohicans.'

He had pawned his fine collection of discs for a mingy sum in order to pay for his slops.

"There's so many conflicting conflagrations in the pipeline," he complained; "I simply don't know who to take on trust." Thinking of entering the church.

Bates immediately paid over his loss after disputing which was the closest star to our duce.

"It's all a matter of suggestion," he announced. "I've erected your chart, and my interpretation is that you are like a *Phoenix* eternally rising up from the bones. Toss it over the shoulder. There's no point crying over spilt knacker-milk," he decreed.

"If you set the great unwashed a bad example," he suggested, "then 'you' pretend that it's they who are totally 'out of order.' The dregs of society are so fucking docile. I wouldn't be surprised if one day even a leading man was elected to become leader of the free world. I've even heard a rumour that there's *already* a bluffer in the Whitehouse."

"You've hit the nail right on my nut."
"Don't give it a moment's thought," nodded Bates. "I've been called all the names under the sun in my time. Look how adeptly I always avoided giving my seminar. There's nowt sa queer as folk," he tittered.

"You should always attempt to hide a portion in the dark. Are you still moonlighting?" he quipped.

"See all, hear all, say nowt!"

He paused for breath and adjusted his quare nippers.
"I've been talking to a chick from the homeground who
used to have the low-down with you," he sniggered.

"Her boyfriend chains her bare arse to the
blistering red hot radiator and screws the hell out of
her! She swears that you were a scruffy little eel at
kindergarten." All shook up!

"She couldn't believe me when I informed her how
much you had burst at the seams. It's a pity she's no
babe." Vassal miscreant! Edge of the known galaxy.

"I've had that recurring dream again!"
He giggled just like 'Willie Carson' riding a flea.

"I dreamt that I was just a shiftless, spineless
Jellyman without any real backbone at all in me... and
that without my complete works of prestidigitation I
wouldn't even appear capable of far-sighted folly, or
voluntary euthanasia. World's so full of shit man."

But it was always difficult to discern if Bates was
just manoevering one of his many sides, and he had
already rebuked the *hoi polloi* more than once for being
too afraid to fib. Mental detecting. *Boings* were
unemployable! Givers or Takers. Which one are you?

The Cock-or-two repeated his story several times and
offered his 'screwed-up' sketch of 'Lucretia Borgia'
with a penis lodged in its cochlea. Once had a brush
with the law. What's hot on the catwalk Tophat?

They discussed the gouache water colour which
someone had presented as part of their final
exhibition; a gnostic metaphor containing an *Oran Utan*
being fellated by a member of the 'Tuatha' as it hung
on the cross at Calvary. Only the good die young!

Underneath its horrid caption, 'Suffer me to come
onto little children;' obviously a biblical allusion
regarding the sacrificial crucifixion and entering into
heaven. *Shunga*...no black without white.

Its effect on the evangelical movement at the
college had been diabolical. Sins of the flesh! Below
the salt. Must have gone through a fortune in tracing-
paper conscientiously objecting. Defended his
intellectual property throughout.

When he ascribed the nature of the thunderbolt the rabble-rouser immediately placed the incident in the realm of holy curse. Well weird! He whistled the incredible demon.

"Hell's broth, I need to make myself scarce!" he jinked in a hotch-potch of alternating pastels.

"But I did warn you not to issue challenges you couldn't hope to cope with many moons later. Only the day after tomorrow belongs to the scumbag."

"That's awful!" he seethed, supining awkwardly in the quiet room and lessening his thud. "He who hesitates is gone forever."

Scales were beginning to spread over his blistering skin. "It's just a normal bodily function like crapping or stuffing your gut with oysters." That orgasm was to the benefit of organisms.

"I do wish you wouldn't burden me with the knowledge of your worsening crises. But now that you have confided in me I promise not to pin it to the door. Never judge a book by its newspaper write-ups. There are times when a man's gotta do what a man's gotta do."

"One must always be aware of the feelings of beatniks," quibbled the side-kick gloomily.

"Money is honey! What a load of baloney" Said his whole existence was in tatters.

"Do you realize?" he gasped. "This could affect the rest of your adult life!" "I don't believe you would..." Safer after the water-shed?

Then he began yapping about the latest advances in technology. The only tool he didn't possess must have been an arse-trimmer. "Hair today gone tomorrow," he cackled. "If you fall from the saddle then quickly remount." Spare me the clod-kicker wisdom.
Mathew divested the *X-certificate* insurrection.

"They're holding a prayer meeting in the chapel at lunchtime today," he grinned. "The *Chaplain* thinks you have an abnormal 'manifestation' which will take some getting rid of...and that you have a peculiar disfiguration on your right side which can only be healed by their devout determination."

"What are you giving up for Lent? Fight fire with a
prick up the bum. That Mr. Wroe had some serious
wickedness in him! There was a time when women were
but two-thirds the size of mortal men. We keep on
getting pegged back," he hammered. "If you can't score
in your twenties. Great hurricanes announce themselves
with but a single breeze."

The idea occurred to ask Bates if he really was
still a creeping encratite, but the thought of
broaching such a sensitive subject with the prickly
Jellyman could easily have rebounded.

He continued with the ongoing charades...
"Mr. and Mrs. Bates were taking their young son along
for his first day at public school to meet his new
headmaster. The young lad was ushered forward by Mr.
Bates and introduced to the harsh disciplinarian in his
capital study..."And this here is young Master Bates,"
said the father to the schoolmaster.

"Don't worry old chum..."
"We'll soon put a stop to that!" chirped the master
sternly, with a wry twirl of his moustache.

"The two-faced back-stabbing bastard!" he hissed.
Had a cynic's eye for logic.

There were questions about Bates that never seemed
to be answered. For instance; did he always wash his
hands after every visit to the lavatory, or before?
Peel slowly and sink your teeth in.

He finally elected to visit the Ferryman.
Apparently *carrot juice only turned his urine orange,*
but the mescaline was increasing his powers of
observation.

J.B. said that he knew of a power plant which could
make him split his britches, but he was better at
keeping things up his sleeve. He suddenly came to his
senses. Treat 'em cruel, make 'em drool!

He always seemed to be on the run.
Said he was more screwed-up than a pen-pusher's reject
slip and it was impossible to turn the clock back.

It was like picking fleas from a dead donkey.
Call him a free-mason, sometimes a green-man, call him
a fool...

Said he'd made a new year's resolution never to make
any more new year's resolutions.

"There, but for the grace of the undying entity go
I," quivered the undeniable Jellyman...

Being of sound mind and body Mathew knew at once that
he couldn't follow where angels feared to tread, so he
disappeared up to the ninth floor, wearing his straight
jacket. Whatever tickles your fancy does you good!

There was bound to be a wraith alone in the changing
room with its large peephole in the broken portal.

A foreign distrust followed his every step from
colleagues who had once been so boot licking. He
needed to put on a face-mask.

Chang gradually approached the mature brunette
chatting on the admin blower until she perlustrated his
rum residence. Snapper of keys in their locks!

She glared at him then smiled. He enquired if there
was a way onto the roof to take some snapshots.

"You'll have to get permission!" snapped the head of
department. "But I'm sure that you will be able to
obtain some good views from the *Rear window* of
Furniture design."

He placed the workchair against the door and began
stripping as she covertly watched him...he panned the
subject with his lens. Cheap thrills. Bodies
throughout the world. Ball-breaker.

Occasionally taking a sip of her Capacino and
doodling on her sketchpad she scrutinized the stunt-
merchant while giving a running commentary. Another
bloody generalization...!

Before occultation eventually elapsed another staff
member appeared from the nearby liftshaft.

Blue Jeans gandered quickly towards him as she
zipped past and tore into the empty L-shaped room to
his left. She floundered at cock level as he moved
more riskily into the open savanna. Place a little
acid in the water supply... bloody great general!

In the twinkling of an eye he was standing
motionless in the corridoor outside the Georgian wiring
of the door glass.

She accidentally nudged the scissure wider and sang her macaronic verse...exposing himself to further serious risk.

Quickly away he returned to his private studio where *Chia Swee* would be bearing fruit next to his own miserable space.

He darted like a whippet between the boardwalks to mount his position behind the huge canvas of Gollum's; a leaning chimney stack breathing smoke across the *Chersonese*.

He opened the filthy rag, the remainder of which had been used as someone's crude exhibit, and reckoned on he was doing some colouring before slowly rotating to see if she was current.

Chia Swee was putting the finishing touches to her admirable desiderata, while the cult of 'Born again' christians chanted away in some long forgotten corner forever banished, gradually rising to a crushing crescendo of *caterwauling*.

Then he stole over to arrange the man-high polythene structure, which was framed with bamboo, to just the right angle. It was a damned nuisance how it was always moved whenever the bird had flown.

He began to expose his skyscraper, peering intensely through the hive, as the *Chink* prepared herself for what was coming.

Her solid eyes grew dark as he edged indecently closer to the webbing, the seedy fabric of which, was the only device separating her untrammelled view from his routine extravaganza.

With his *glistening lens* he snapped her hazy sockets through the transparent screen of kite.

Suddenly Geraldine appeared at her side and began integrating her *pastiche*.

Both students studied hard while Geraldine repeatedly stroked her eyebrow. From tiny ejaculations mighty pontiff's do appear!

She bit her desirable scarlet lip in a southerly direction, to extend his *temporary bliss*.

Pain in the arse of the cantankerous old git!

Her chaperon glazed over as the blonde peered over to obtain a better compass, his geyser spurted into the upper chamber...and the eye of the voyeur quickly scarpered from the vantage point, on hearing the group of students perambulating closer.

He coolly rubbed the sticky moisture into the sawdust and ground his cowboy booted heel.

The overtrick of his emission he touched up on the back of the brushwork, which was the only article separating him from *complete notoriety*.

Too late cracking the whip after the horse had bolted! He wore the purple.

"It's a septic tank of loathsome poison!" sneered a voice only centimetres away and blocking his flight path.

As he arrived down the driveway he met *Griselda* taking her poodle, Mitzy, for a walk towards the Blackheath.

The old retired 'factories inspector' stopped to reminisce for a while before submitting her treatise on the sterility of public office.

Some git had rung college to say that he had been found gagged to a chair with his throat slashed.

"How many times did I see her slouching at my gate," she said. "Holding her head in her hands and not wishing to go home just yet." Must have had a real ding-donger. Something Mathew had said.

On *tulip court* Lindsey was swaggering in the middle of the road with her fresh band of onlookers.

As his *lambswool* bobble flopped from side to side the jeering would begin in earnest as he crossed to the sunny side of the street. Eat more spinach!

She called for a French-Letter, but beauty was said to be only skin deep. His purple-pronged-penis!

His heart beat like a miner's recant to the sound of tearing straw but he still wasn't climbing in the car with a treacherous crimp. Plead for a clean break.

"Flash, Flasher!" hollered the new recruits from the fence. "Why don't you get a hair transplant?" they imparted. A pedestrian with wheels on his toes.

"She's got more hair underneath her armpits than you have on your baldy head."

But he still possessed her last Valentine's card of a 'Partridge in a pear tree.' Called him a Big Puff!

"There's plenty more fishes in the sea...Julie's a nice respectable girl," said his mother calmly.

"You're like a blackbird striving to be a peacock." "She would like to arrange a date for tomorrow evening. Why don't you take her to the flicks when she comes around for brunch? She puts that other girl in the shade."

"She's too plain and dull!" he said. "Far too conventional for my outlandish tastes. I'd prefer someone more provocative, rather than a frustrated window dresser afraid of being left on the shelf..."

Conveniently, her mother emerged to hang the dirty linen, when the pin-pricks had left the neighbourhood.

Just as Mollydod was passing the entrance Mathew lightly entered the old pumping-house in his swimming trunks and nothing else.

Conducting a pleasant conversation over the ha-ha he stood on tip-toe to see if it really was a hair-piece...loyal to the past was one thing.

Working her way tirelessly around the ledges the older woman eventually kneeled to water the greenhouse plants of her potting shed, exactly opposite the plotting magenta faced pumper frozen in the door hole.

Through the wicker fence the *Vickerman* focused on her browless buds to be sure that they were observing him...they frequently gagged, but seemed on the whole to be rather like whirlpools.

A purple glow-worm shining incandescently above reflected on the window glass to highlight his star attraction, as he peeled away his splendid foam-flecked nakedness and his bell-end glittered magnificently from the plat. The smeared ambrosia of his cloth.

She loitered supererrogatively round the base of the shaft tending and nurturing the stalks, as his erect penis phosphored in her medium brown eyes growing dim.

At regular intervals she tipped her eager spout to moisten her prospering sprigs with her cloudy eyes occasionally watering.

As his penis proudly prodded the late afternoon weather-wise and began to spurt fresh semen on the wind *Griselda* commenced her croon of *Gilbert and Sullivan* at the top of her lungs, and made up her mind never to flinch from the organ of vision. Kojak's revenge!

He fried to a frizzle under the boiling acid. By the time he was due to retire his body was like a blackened bonfire twig...

In the kitchen her *Shout* magazine lay open in its usual place on the sideboard...

Unfaltering in her bond she climbed the stairs to freedom when no concrete answer came.

Below him in the pot was one of Mary's soiled tampons which she had scrupulously omitted to flush.

Every other step she trod Caroline called out anxiously to discern if he was really in the house or just a pussy obnoxious twat.

"Mathew are you there?" she tremoured, as her hand crept over the squeaky bannister rail, mixed with increased suspense and mouth-watering anticipation.

"Hello?" she asked again...standing white faced before the full length mirror.

"Is anybody there? What are you doing now?" Not a word in reply did the deviant utter, as she paused good manneredly before turning the brow...

Her long golden threads began to edge around the wooden surface, above her sultry smile.

Should he let her into his cranny? He was seriously winded.

One more step and she would have a blockbuster to particularize to her peerage.

"Are you there?" she brayed in a weak and yearning tone, awaiting a reply, but none arrived.

Mathew quickly slammed the door shut and began doing up his flies. Too much flare makes a desert.

Appearing from the restricted cubicle minutes later he still found her face an absolute disgrace.

"Don't you ever creep up on me like that again!" he angrily rebuked her.

"Never come upstairs unless you have a permit," he nervously chastised...She looked like the morning sun, but he could not remember.

She was as cold as December, F. could not forget what she had done...

But if broad daylight scoured his eyes then welcome night was his happy home!

For hours he waited at the side of the kerb and managed to follow the blue saloon into the brushwood.

The motor cruised along the road and then turned into the wooded grove below the plague of houses.

Parked at the top of the spinney he maundered while the goose was dressed.

He carefully unfolded his *Gannex raincoat* from the duffel-bag and closed his door quietly on the catch, before quaking to the 'hawking grounds' of the heath, like a killer on the loose.

It was during a particularily dense spica of gloom that he paced up and down the wicket, where he could stand in their grotto to watch them through the awning envelope...the *Night hunter!*

In the summerhouse a frequent visitor trotted to discharge a solitary muezzin's cry, unaware that a disturbed person was loitering in her vicinity exorcising his compulsory tendency.

The eldest boy seemed to be completely 'under her thumb...' His earth fell through the skies.

Venturing over to the living room of *the house with yellow brick* the stumbling Tom drooped through to the narrow chink of light, which seeped past the window blind near to his 'Argus.'

He perlustrated her in close proximity for the first time in light years, contemplating how clearly she had bloomed in the intervening period.

"You will do it!" she screamed at the older child.

"You will do as you are told at once and switch it off to come and play with me."

Her wide pink lips were prettily covered with fresh make-up as she kneeled between his straddled legs and ordered him to snog the entrance to Paradise.

Suddenly she gobbed in the ashtray.
There was a growl and her eyes sky-dived towards the fracture. She leapt to her feet intending to investigate further. The sun fell in his shoes.

"Who is it?" she called to the terrier. "See if you can find the dirty rotten scoundrel."

I only knew what hunted thought quickened his step and why, he looked upon the garish sky with such a wistful eye. My sunshine, my sweetheart, my rain...

Is there anything you'd like me to do?
"Stand a little out of my Sun!"
Smiled the *Vickerman*.

"I could have been great with someone, and someone could have been great with me."

Biography

Born in West Yorkshire, progeny of an English Schoolteacher and an Irish wolfhound.
Worked as an Art therapist, Football referee, and teacher of Sign-language.
Currently runs a creative writing workshop in Norfolk.
Award winning poet and short story writer.
Trained Astrologer and former body-builder.
Social Commentator of world-renown. Magic carpet restorer. Campaigner for Tourette's.
In 2007 was caught in possession of a First World War Browning revolver which had once belonged to Field Marshal Erwin Rommel, but did not intend to murder anyone with it.
Once taught Boris Johnson how to throw a welly.
Staunch believer in Universal freedom; the obligation to question, especially those with received authority, and the rights of the individual over and above that of the State.
Strong opponent of political correctness and Government eunuchs with the upper storey missing.

* BANNED FROM LIBRARIES AND KNOCKING-SHOPS UP AND DOWN THE COUNTRY.

Also by the same Author on AMAZON uk: Hrothgar's lost parchments.
Thunderbuck Ram I, 3 &4 (The Changeling, Grendel Returns, Fimbulwinter).
Dada's final Gallery. Dance of the red-crowned Prince.
BUNDERCHOOK STARWORD POET

Completely off my rocker

ə⌒ ∴ ⩳ ≑≑---- ⩳ ♩ ♋ ◡̇ Ĝ≒⌒ ≑◡̇ ∘ ---- ♥ ↗↘屄 ▪ ---- ▪
⩳↘⌒̇Ĝ⩳↘⌒̇ ≒⌒ ⩳‴ ----◡̇ ✕ ▪ ♩ ♋◡̇----Ĝ♥✕ ▪ ♋ ▪
♋‴ ↗∴∴✕↘ ∘ ‴ ↗⁂↘⌒̇ ≒⌒ ⩳↘∓≑◡̇----ḣ ú ♮ ✕
⌒̇ ∘ ◡̇ ▪ ≑✕∓◡̇ ⩳ ⌒̇‴ ⁂ ∘ ⩳⌒̇⌒̇✕♩ ▪ ♥✕ ▪ ♋ ♩
‴ ⩳∴---- ✕↘ ∴↗ ▪ ♋ ≒⌒ ♋✕ √----ḣ í↗‴ ▪ ♥◡̇≑⁂
◡̇ ♋↗⁂‴ ---- ◡̇⁂◡̇ ‴ ⌒ ↘✕ ∘ ♋ ▪ ú ♩ ⩳↘屄 ▪ ∘ ◡̇ ▪
▪ ↗ ----≑◡̇◡̇ √ḣ ú ♮ ≒⌒ ♩ ♋◡̇---- ▪ ⌒̇↗◡̇----↘屄 ▪ √
‴ ✕ ♩ ∓ ≒⌒ ♋◡̇⩳⌒̇⩳ ♩ ♋◡̇ ♩ ↗≒◡̇----Ĝ⩳↘⌒̇ ú ♥
✕≑≑ ↘◡̇⁂◡̇‴ ♮ ✕↘✕----♋ ✕ ▪ ⩳≑≑ ✕↘ ▪ ✕≒
◡̇ḣ

“It was a long time coming” Harvey ■■ ▬ ■ ■ ■■ ▬ ■

Disgusting, ghastly and extremely unpleasant. Should have had a doctor to treat his acne years ago!

HOT AIR

MUM

By Adumla | Published: October 8, 2017 | Edit

Turned the router to face the window so I couldn't see she had broken my connection.

Some people never change!

Webbo

By Adumla | Published: October 8, 2017 | Edit

Wrote to Webbo and the gang tonight to confirm my new identities and say that I have never been a malicious person capable of harm.

Castration of the Catalan Government

By Sarin | Published: November 3, 2017 | Edit

This is just the wrong time of year to try to gain independence. You just can't go around having free democratic elections if we don't like it. (As the United Kingdom discovered; Central Government will try and get their own back if you want to run your own affairs). The only people allowed to bear arms are those in power!

Judges will always obey their paymasters

You can get locked up just for speaking your mind

A *European arrest warrant* will be issued

I heard one observer comment that it was all:

"Politically motivated!" You don't say?

Annual Christian Business-man's dinner

By Sarin | Published: November 3, 2017 | Edit

- Free to all who pay
- Come and have your brain fire-hosed
- Meet with like-minded con artists
- Smother yourself with Carols
- Eat with the rich and not so poor
- Better than watching Corrie
- Good for your soul

You will be invited back another time just so long as you agree to toe-the-line.

Fallon witch-hunt

By HERPES ZOSTER | *Published: NOVEMBER 2, 2017* | *Edit*

"He touched her knee 'inappropriately,' and said 'how about putting those nice cold little handies somewhere lovely and warm?"
You two faced mealy-mouthed Wankers of Great Britain!

Baby sawn in two

By HERPES ZOSTER | Published: NOVEMBER 2, 2017 | Edit

To keep a young infant alive doctors were forced to hack off its limbs and remove a hand. Has society gone mad or is it just the same Nannies in Authority who think this is right?

Labels on everything

By Sarin | Published: November 3, 2017 | Edit

Mum has taken to putting labels on everything. Not just her pots and pans but her knives and forks as well.
She finished putting my label on years ago…
The smell of her clothes soaking in the sink is making me puke!
I finally found out why she had been searching for the phone manual.
"Of course, you can ring her. You can phone her anytime you like. It doesn't cost me a penny."
The bitch has blocked me ringing my partner to tell her I am back home safely each night.
I'm expecting more of this as my Aunt and Uncle's visit approaches.
When they get here I bet you they won't even speak to me once and I will remain safely shut in my room.

. ···**cs,**·
.

I did re-submit 7779561 with a full bleed. I don't understand why it keeps getting rejected. Do you? Are there any Christians on the staff…I am beginning to suspect some kind of conspiracy…

I wrote to say that page 54 (for instance) *did not* have any writing missing, but they still rejected it on that grounds. It was fine the way it was.

These Technicians are certainly not artists. The whole idea of art is to break with tradition.

If it really makes them happy I will align page 54 to look like the rest and alter the size of the back-page print.

. ▬ · ·· ▬ ▪▪

The Author

Kevin Spacey…surely not?

By GODFREY WINKLEBACKER | *Published: NOVEMBER 9, 2017* | *Edit*

Scenes removed from films. Characters eradicated from books. People we don't like or know scrubbed away from the offending location.
TRIAL BE MEDIA.
What gleaming greedy Politician is going to disagree with that?

RESPECT! *By* GODFREY WINKLEBACKER | *Published: NOVEMBER 9, 2017* | *Edit*

Chris rang Brian to ask how his appointment with the Doctor went.
He dropped the phone. Said he was too busy to speak. He said his credit had
run out. Didn't bother to ring back as he promised again.
"She is my grand-daughter…"
Too busy on his X-box!
Can't believe a single word they say.
The alleged 'lung-infection' had cleared up, but Yvonne still had to throw her job
in at work.
"Brian's too poorly to look after his little girl."
"They're putting me under too much stress mum!"
"She's a fat slob!" hissed Chris. "I never want anything to do with her."
"She would rather lose her job than let Sophia stay five minutes with me."

Comments

Radicalization by non-Muslims

By GODFREY WINKLEBACKER | *Published: NOVEMBER 9, 2017* | *Edit*

Governments never lie. They never bitch on each other!
There is never any bitching or back-stabbbing.
Everyone should join together for the good of the party.
We let her fall on her sword. It was the right thing to do.
(We wanted rid of her anyway).
We never *really* knew she was seeing the Jews.

'More animal semen needed to expand the production of endangered species'
Albert Cameranus Grimshaw: Grassy Farm land, Widdock, Peak District Nark.

'More steel toe-caps and truncheons required'

Lord William Butler-Fright: Bring it to me soon, Birmingham.

'We no longer believe in the Divine Right of Kings'

Seamus 'Queen' O'Malley: Black-and-Tan the Bosh, Chamber Maid, No-Stormont, IRELAND.

'Want a job? Accuse your boss of sexual harassment.'

Tracey Saxe-Coburg Gotha: TELL-TALES-R-THE-BEST, Country Shires Model Agency, Woking, SURREY.

'Abuse of power: we don't believe in it'

Tony Knob-Head Duke: Pubic Games and Landowners Association, PLYMOUTH HOE.

'All I have to do now is decide whether to buy a new Star War's outfit or the
recent Lego castle edition'
Michael Birdseye: Council Ruffian, Scrounger, No Works Road, YAKIDAH CITY.

'Too lazy to breastfeed. Would rather play on her mobile phone than do any housework.'
Susan Birdseye: **Parent & Grandparent, Brick-through-the-window, Rough Council Estate. Wales.**

'Hi handsome. Love from me xxxxx' August 2017
Linda Hartley: Housewife, HUDDERSFIELD.

The End

Printed in Great Britain
by Amazon

48060283R00086